T0358711

A Performatory Approach to Teaching, Learning and Technology

Bold Visions in Educational Research
Volume 34

Series Editors:
Kenneth Tobin, *The Graduate Center, City University of New York, USA*
Joe Kincheloe, *McGill University, Montreal, Canada*

Editorial Board:
Heinz Sunker, *Universität Wuppertal, Germany*
Peter McLaren, *University of California at Los Angeles, USA*
Kiwan Sung, *Woosong University, South Korea*
Angela Calabrese Barton, *Teachers College, New York, USA*
Margery Osborne, *Centre for Research on Pedagogy and Practice Nanyang Technical*
University, Singapore
W.-M. Roth, *University of Victoria, Canada*

Scope:
Bold Visions in Educational Research is international in scope and includes books from two areas: *teaching and learning to teach* and *research methods in education.* Each area contains multi-authored handbooks of approximately 200,000 words and monographs (authored and edited collections) of approximately 130,000 words. All books are scholarly, written to engage specified readers and catalyze changes in policies and practices. Defining characteristics of books in the series are their explicit uses of theory and associated methodologies to address important problems. We invite books from across a theoretical and methodological spectrum from scholars employing quantitative, statistical, experimental, ethnographic, semiotic, hermeneutic, historical, ethnomethodological, phenomenological, case studies, action, cultural studies, content analysis, rhetorical, deconstructive, critical, literary, aesthetic and other research methods.

Books on *teaching and learning to teach* focus on any of the curriculum areas (e.g., literacy, science, mathematics, social science), in and out of school settings, and points along the age continuum (pre K to adult). The purpose of books on *research methods in education* is **not** to present generalized and abstract procedures but to show how research is undertaken, highlighting the particulars that pertain to a study. Each book brings to the foreground those details that must be considered at every step on the way to doing a good study. The goal is **not** to show how generalizable methods are but to present rich descriptions to show how research is enacted. The books focus on methodology, within a context of substantive results so that methods, theory, and the processes leading to empirical analyses and outcomes are juxtaposed. In this way method is not reified, but is explored within well-described contexts and the emergent research outcomes. Three illustrative examples of books are those that allow proponents of particular perspectives to interact and debate, comprehensive handbooks where leading scholars explore particular genres of inquiry in detail, and introductory texts to particular educational research methods/issues of interest. to novice researchers.

A Performatory Approach to Teaching, Learning and Technology

Jaime E. Martinez

SENSE PUBLISHERS
ROTTERDAM/BOSTON/TAIPEI

A C.I.P. record for this book is available from the Library of Congress.

ISBN: 978-94-6091-664-9 (paperback)
ISBN: 978-94-6091-665-6 (hardback)
ISBN: 978-94-6091-666-3 (e-book)

Published by: Sense Publishers,
P.O. Box 21858,
3001 AW Rotterdam,
The Netherlands
www.sensepublishers.com

Printed on acid-free paper

TABLE OF CONTENTS

FOREWORD

I have a young friend (he's currently four) and while I am not sure what his first word was, his first two-word phrase was, "GooGoo budozer" (Translation: Google bulldozer). Before he could even walk he would crawl under my chair and pull out my laptop, that I had hoped to put out of his reach, and push it towards me saying, "GooGoo budozer," which was my cue to search on Google Images for photographs of hundreds of bulldozers…followed by dumptrucks, cranes, and construction vehicles I had never even heard of. By two he was playing *Angry Birds,* and landing airplanes and helicopters on his mama's iPhone, and at three and a half he had successfully used Youtube videos to learn all the words to the songs *Aquarius* and *Camptown Races*. By now he is an experienced internet researcher and when I tell him that I don't know the answer to one of his infinite *"Why?"* questions he takes us over to the computer to find the answer.

My friend learned to do all of this without a single traditional lesson, not unlike how he learned to walk, talk, sit up at the dinner table and ride the subway (another one of his fascinations). Long before he could actually manipulate the mouse or hold the phone to his ear the adults around him related to him as a becoming member of a technology using species. And over the course of many experiences he quickly became not only a member, but also someone who is beginning to show *us* how to utilize technology in new ways.

Flash-forward four years into an imagined future and my friend, now age 8, is starting the third grade. His classroom has two computers, but they are 5 years old and they often crash when the children try to run anything other than the word processing program. Moreover, his teacher describes herself as "not very good with technology," and the computers are rarely used during ordinary lessons. However, the school has received a grant to hire a technology teacher and from third grade on each class receives one hour of instruction a week.

Imagine that today is my friend's first day of computer class. He and his classmates walk excitedly into the "lab" where there are 30 computers sitting a top traditional desks and facing the front of the room. As soon as the children sit down they start to play with the computers. Some children, like my friend, appear to have a great deal of experience and they start to show the others how to get started. The teacher quickly claps his hands and says, "All eyes on me and hands in your laps." He tells them to sit quietly with their hands folded while he explains the rules of the classroom. For the next 20 minutes he talks about what they are *not* allowed to do (touch the computers without permission, share computers without permission, explore the internet without permission, or go to certain programs that are reserved for the upper grades). After these warnings he announces that he is going to begin by teaching them how to work the computers and he turns on a projector and starts an animated film on what a computer is …

We are at an interesting moment in the field of education. For centuries learning and schooling have been almost synonymous. Over time, with the advent of capitalism and industrialization there was a move away from the informal learning that had previously happened in fields and kitchens, or the semi-formal apprenticeship model of workshops and clerk offices, towards a form of learning that separated children from adult work, and made learning a prerequisite to doing. There have been great gains made by that shift for children in particular and humanity in general—a much more literate population, a safer and more humane place for children to spend their days, and an opportunity for families to move up the class ladder by having access to higher paid jobs.

However, there is also evidence that schools are failing to be a place of learning for large numbers of children, particularly poor children and children of color. The high school graduation rate for the country hovers around 75%, but for African-Americans it is 62% (Rampell, 2010, June 2), and for African-American males it's reported as below 50% (Schott Foundation, 2008). In addition in the key subjects of math and reading some reports show 48% of African Americans and 43% of Latino students as "below basic" (McKinsey and Co., 2009).

While schools appear to be declining in effectiveness it is also the case that there is an explosion of innovations happening in the field of teaching and learning, almost all outside of school, and many of them making use of the continuous technological revolution we are in. There is evidence that the most innovative, most effective, and just most interesting teaching and learning is happening outside of schools. All one has to do is watch any number of TED (Technology, Entertainment and Design) Talks to see that there is no shortage of wonderful ideas and projects springing up that make use of children's fascination with technology, and give children and youth opportunities to be in contact with people and ideas from around the world, in other words that make their worlds bigger and support them to develop as learners (Holzman, 2009; Lobman, 2011).

I am a fan of these TED Talks, the 20-minute videos that feature people talking about almost anything that has a ring of innovation or creativity. As a lifelong educator, my favorite ones have to do with learning (see Mitra, 2010 or Robinson, 2006). I am also a proponent and researcher of outside of school programs, many of which have been very successful in supporting the growth and development of young people (Heath, 2000; Lobman, 2011; Vadeboncoeur, 2006). If you watch enough of these videos or explore the world of outside of school programming *and* you spend time in schools a disturbing realization begins to emerge. There is a huge gap between the amount, type, and quality of the ideas and practices that exist in the world, and that are actually working to transform the learning lives of children and adults, even those living in remote places and under impoverished conditions, and what is happening in many classrooms of the richest country in the world. Schools, the place where most children are expected to do most of their learning, are often the least effective environments for doing just that.

There are a lot of things one could do about that, including despair. Or give up on the six or seven hours children spend in school and concentrate entirely on their outside of school time. However, there are other choices, and in *A Performatory Approach to Teaching, Learning, and Technology* Jaime Martinez shows us one of them. Martinez came out of the world of business technology and, after a successful career; he chose to become a teacher in order to give his expertise to the next generation. Then, when he was confronted with the realities of inner city schools, he did not despair, instead he did what teachers have to do in a broken system—create with what you have, with the emphasis being on create.

In *A Performatory Approach to Teaching, Learning, and Technology*, Martinez shares how he has been able to bring the kind of creative, innovative, and rigorous learning that is happening outside of school into his (and others) public school classrooms. And he shares it in a way that is accessible, playful, and most of all real. In the stories that he tells there are no illusions about what life in schools is like, but by sharing what he was been able to accomplish he puts a demand on teachers to recognize that they are not just *in school* they are also *in the world.* And the world offers multiple approaches to learning, many of which are more effective for developing young people as learners than the dominant model.

Throughout the book Martinez shares a variety of classes that he has worked with. What these stories have in common is that, whether in the South Bronx, New Jersey, or Manhattan, Martinez and the children are performing as technology experts and in the course of that their expertise is able to develop. One could argue he is not so much teaching technology, as he is modeling/teaching an approach to learning--an approach that does not separate learning from the creating of the environment for learning. When I read this book it gave me hope. Hope for the hundreds of children that have been taught by Martinez, hope for the thousands upon thousands of students of the teachers who will read this book, and hope for my young friend, who I want to continue to relate to technology as one of his many playthings.

Carrie Lobman
Associate Professor
Graduate School of Education
Rutgers, The State University of New Jersey
10 Seminary Place
New Brunswick, NJ 08901

REFERENCES

Heath, S. (2000). Making learning work. *Afterschool Matters, 1*(1), 33–45.

Kurlander, G., & Fulani, L. (2009). *Achievement gap or development gap? "Outliers" and outsiders reconsider an old problem.* New York: All Stars Project, Inc.

Lobman, C. (2011). Democracy and development: The role of outside of school experiences in preparing young people to be active citizens. *Democracy and Education, 19*(1). Retrieved from http://democracyeducationjournal.org

McKinsey & Co. (2009). *The economic impact of the achievement gap in America's schools.* New York: McKinsey & Co Social Sector Office.

Mitra, S. (2010, July). *Suguta Mitra: The child driven curriculum.* Retrieved from http://www.ted.com/talks/sugata_mitra_the_child_driven_education.html

Rampell, C. (2010, June 2). Graduation rates by state and race. *New York Times Economix.* Retrieved from http://economix.blogs.nytimes.com/2010/06/02/graduation-rates-by-state-and-race/

FOREWORD

Robinson, K. (2006, February). *Ken Robinson says schools kill creativity.* Retrieved from http://www.ted.com/talks/ken_robinson_says_schools_kill_creativity.html

Schott Foundation. (2008). *Given half a chance: The Schott 50 state report on public education and black males.* Cambridge, MA: Schott Foundation for Public Education. Retrieved from http://www.blackboysreport.org/files/schott50statereport-execsummary.pdf

Vadeboncoeur, J. (2006). Engaging young people: Learning in informal context. *Review of Research in Education, 30,* 239–78.

ACKNOWLEDGEMENTS

My thanks and gratitude to the following people and groups of people:

For creating the environments where I could learn and develop - Lois Holzman, Carrie Lobman, Gwen Lowenheim and the staff and faculty at the East Side Institute for Group and Short Term Psychotherapy.

For creating the opportunity for adults to re-initiate development while supporting young people – Lenora Fulani, Pam Lewis and the staff of the All Stars Project.

For helping and supporting my work without colonizing me - Ken Tobin

For being my friends and colleagues in all the different environments that I've learned, worked, and laughed in – you know who you are.

For their work on the cover art – Jessie Martinez and Bernard Nazario

For being my family – Migdalia, Jessie, Mami, Papi, Connie, Christy, Cheli and all my nieces and nephews.

WORKING WITH WHAT THERE IS

AN INTRODUCTION

This book is about becoming a better teacher. For me, that process included learning to take responsibility for creating learning environments. In doing so, I developed as a leader and I learned to support the development of others by working with groups. My history as a technology professional, philanthropist and New York City Teaching Fellow generated my interests in creating learning environments in public schools. There are very specific meanings that I attach to the phrase "creating learning environments" that will be explored at length.

The audience for this book includes urban educators in teacher preparation programs and first year doctoral students with an interest in incorporating technology into teaching and learning activities. If you don't happen to be in graduate school, but you are interested in a cutting edge educational practice, this book is for you as well. The narratives and vignettes illustrate life in school and the theory behind my pedagogical approach is grounded in experience. Hopefully, that will make what is being presented accessible to someone who is not in graduate school. While this is not a "how to" book and there are no methods or lesson plans, you will get a practitioner's view on how to create new possibilities in a technology rich classroom. Undergraduate students and practitioners who have been in the classroom for a few years may feel challenged by some of the terminology and theory. I've included a glossary, chapter highlights and questions for extra support.

My teaching practice integrates technology into instruction using a collaborative performance-based approach to teaching and learning. What does performance have to do with technology? Well, that's what the rest of this book is about. I'll start by stating that I have learned that we are all performers and we can use our capacity to perform to change ourselves and to change the social scenes we live in. This discovery has turned out to be very useful in my attempts to create positive learning environments for my students and myself. My process for becoming a better teacher also included teaching in public schools, examining my uses of technology, working with others in diverse settings, earning a Ph.D., and creating this book.

Ethnography, in social science, is a description of the lives, events and customs of people that has some scientific rigor to it. The stories, vignettes and scenes in ethnography should be plausible and peers should be able to verify the authenticity of the narratives. An ethnography describes life as it unfolds, the reader may at times wonder why I tell a certain story at a certain time in an effort to see the logic of what I am presenting. Logic gives you a particular way to see things, in this book, I am asking you to see things differently than you may normally do.

In this auto-ethnography, the stories that I tell about my life as an educator unfolded in this book in a particular way. I am telling the stories in the context of creating a book. I might tell them differently if I am working side by side with you in a school or swapping war stories over beers in a bar. Context matters to the storyteller and to the audience. This book kept changing as I kept living my life and new ideas occurred to me. I wanted to produce a book that shares my teaching practice and is also good social science.

If you wanted to identify where I was coming from, as a scholar and researcher the answer would be "he's a postmodernist." What that means in practice is that I use other postmodernist scholars and their work to inform my own. If you look up "postmodernism" you will find various definitions that describe postmodernism as a critique of "modernism" and the "grand narrative" and a movement away from "objective truth" and scientific categories.

The scientific method and the scientific categories are tools that human beings have used to change everything in our world. The scientific method is extremely useful in the natural sciences and those methods have become embedded in how we think about the world and the things in it. Logic, as I mentioned previously, is another one of those tools. The methods of science and logic are so much a part of Western culture that we have to make a conscious effort to use other, non-scientific tools to view and interact with the world. In creating an ethnographic account of events in my life I've gotten to experience the tension between doing good science and telling a good story about the lives of people and their experiences. Ethnography does not attempt to provide big theories about how things work; it is a creative attempt to describe what happened and provides an opportunity to reflect on what happened. It is a new kind of tool that has helped me to look at things differently.

My experience has been that writing, reflection and sharing are transformative and have helped with producing changes in the classroom. Play, performance, improvisation and art are examples of other kinds of useful tools that can be used in learning and in the creation of culture that are not scientific. These imaginative and creative tools, like science and logic, have also had a transformative effect my approach to teaching and learning. These are also powerful tools that have changed the world and everything in it. I believe that computer technology is the tool of the 21st century that is most encompassing of all of the other tools that we employ. With computer technology we do what we did before better and faster and we can build things today that we could only imagine in science fiction in the 19th and 20th centuries. Human beings, play, perform, create art, do science, predict weather, build, and communicate using computer technology. There is no question in my mind that computer technology will also be central to how we do teaching and learning in the 21st century. My technology bias is evident, but I am not arguing for technology, I am arguing for teaching and learning practices that incorporate the cultural tools of the moment so that the activity of teaching and learning is culturally relevant to the lives of students and teachers.

A Career Change

For better part of 20 years in my life, I earned a living doing various kinds of work as computer technology professional working in Wall Street financial institutions and a variety of companies located in the greater New York area. I've done everything from tech support to network manager, to programmer/analyst to quality assurance tester. In the late 1990s I was a partner and managing director in my own dot-com venture. When the venture failed, I applied to become a New York City Teaching Fellow and I started teaching in the South Bronx. My idea was that I could teach kids about computer technology and that given all my experience I would be a highly respected and valued teacher, it would be fun and easy.

Things didn't work out exactly that way, but I think they turned out well enough. I learned to be a classroom teacher and started to understand school from the vantage point of an adult insider. With a little encouragement from a mentor, I enrolled in a Ph.D. program and learned about teaching and learning from a different perspective. I became interested in how my uses of technology with students seemed to create a different way of relating to others and different kind of learning activity in the classroom.

I've come to believe that what is needed is an approach to pedagogy that can be responsive to the demand that school-based learning must include integrated uses of digital media and technology. This approach must also address the belief that students may "know more" about technology than some of their teachers. I believe that using theatrical performance and improvisation as part of a methodology that focuses on creating collaborative learning environments can transform the teaching and learning that happens in schools. In the next section I describe what my classroom looked like using this methodology.

WELCOME TO JIM'S TECH CLASS

There is a large beige metal cart in the corner of the room near the door. The doors of the cart are partially open and laptops and electrical power cables can be seen inside. The large windows on the wall opposite the door are shaded against the sun in the southern sky. The small science classroom we are in has bulletin boards covered with student work. There are many plants and animal cages along the windowsills and the bookcases in the back of the room. There is a white board at the front of the room and a wall mounted SMART board at the back of the room. There are fluorescent lights overhead and a clothesline with chart paper hanging by clothespins that detail the various aspects of the scientific method and science writing conventions that students should know. Students are sitting at beige wood patterned rectangular desks organized in groups of four around the room as they sit in pairs and threesomes. Their heads lean in towards each other as they look at the LCD (liquid crystal display) screens on the gray DELL laptops in front of them. One student in each group takes on the chore of typing while his or her partner or partners look on. The room is warm and the windows are open, the sounds of

New York City traffic and children playing outside in the courtyard can be heard. Inside the room is noisy. It is the same kind of energetic chaotic noise many teachers come to associate with environments where collaborative learning is going on. There are usually no noises that are distinguishable from any other, just a babble that rises and falls according to some unknown tempo. On this occasion a student discovers a sound effect in the Microsoft PowerPoint application, the entire room goes silent as the sound of shrill beeping fades in our ears. Smiles, looks of surprise and a collective turning toward the noise follow. Some students will walk to the source of the noise and ask the noisemakers how to make that sound. Others will look at me to check my reaction. The students find that I have resumed talking to a student that I was working with and they go back to their activities.

I finish talking to one student and look around, I spot a raised hand and I make my way across the room. I don't know how long the hand has been up. It might have gone up in response to my straightening up after I left the last student or it may have just been there, waiting for me. Some students will walk up to me and wait for my attention, others will tap me on the shoulder, and some will just start talking in my ear as I am leaning over a computer and working with someone else. As I navigate around chairs and over book bags in the crowded room I check to see what is on the computer screens as I pass. As I reach the student she absently looks up at me and says "Never mind, I just figured it out." I say, "Good!" and I continue to look around and move about the room.

"Too much text! Try using the bullet points and find more pictures."

"That slide looks good, but the font is too small, click over there on that A button and increase the font size."

"The color of the text needs to be darker if you want to be able to see it against that background."

A student walks up to me and asks if I know how to animate the text on a slide. I point her in the direction of some boys who have been successful in doing that and I suggest that she get their help. She goes away and returns seconds later. I keep forgetting that it's still very early in the school year. I stop the classroom. "Ladies and gentlemen, I would like you to keep in mind that what goes on in this class is not a competition. I like it when you help each other. I count on it, and I reward you for it. If someone comes looking for your help, please give it. If you see that someone needs help, please offer it. Okay, everyone go back to work." A few minutes later she draws my attention and shows me her animated text, she seems very pleased. I walk over to the boys who helped and thank them for their efforts.

I still don't know all their names but I'm starting to remember the patterns, certain boys always sit together as do certain girls. Certain kids, whose names I do know, are generating the loudest noises. Certain classes are working faster than others, some work quieter and some are collectively doing higher quality work. It's still early in the year and there is still no consensus among the 6th grade teachers as to which class is the easiest, best or worst.

It's time to get them ready to leave. I announce the 5-minute warning and ask the students to save their files to memory sticks or USB drives (universal serial bus storage devices). It's a new skill and several of the students still haven't become confident or competent at it. Some have already lost files that they "thought we had saved." There's nothing like a student losing a few files to reinforce paying attention when I walk him through saving the current file.

The room becomes hectic, as students start moving around to return laptops to the laptop cart. I start responding to some of the more panicked students who ignored the previous warning and are only now realizing that they aren't quite sure how to save a file. Students are now packing up their large backpacks and traffic around the door is starting to gather and interfere with putting laptops away. I dismiss everyone who is ready to go and the traffic jam near the door abates as I help the students who have been slow to save files. Pretty soon saving files and getting out of the room will be a well-established routine and I won't give them a 5-minute warning 15 minutes before the end of class. September is always frustrating; I have to spend a lot of time on the routines. When my students leave in June they are able to save work, shutdown computers, put them away and leave the room in about 7 minutes.

It Looks The Same… And It Isn't

"It looks the same!" exclaimed my friend and mentor Professor Carrie Lobman from the school of Education at Rutgers as she ate lunch with me after a visit to my classroom in Manhattan. What "It looks the same!" refers to is her prior visit to my computer lab in the South Bronx elementary school two years earlier. During her South Bronx visit she observed me working with 1st graders and 6th graders. These students were considered academically at-risk and were attending a school that was listed as SINI (School In Need of Improvement) by New York State. I can recall that in the 6th grade class she observed there were many students who were not doing the assigned task or were "off task" and resisted my attempts to get them "on task." Off task activities such as games, music lyric websites, and social networking sites, seemed to produce the same leaning in postures, noise levels, collaboration, and enthusiasm that students who are willingly engaged in "on task" activities generate. In other words, in my technology class, playing on computers in the South Bronx looked and sounded a lot like rigorous project work in Manhattan.

Finding Meaningful Work

In the South Bronx I was able to engage student interest by encouraging the activity of creating something by using technology. The technology provided a means to find something that was meaningful to the student in that particular moment. A brief conversation with a student in the South Bronx illustrates the point.

"What kind of PowerPoint presentation would you like to do?"

"I don't know."

"Is there anything that you are interested in?"

"No."

"Is there any place that you would like to go to or see?'

"Hawaii!"

"Okay, why don't we do an Internet search and find some pictures of Hawaii and then you can make your PowerPoint presentation about Hawaii."

"Okay. How do I do that?"

"I'll show you."

I recall that Lobman and I talked about that exchange, we were both surprised at how animated the student had become when she said "Hawaii!" Her level of enthusiasm to do something had been transformed as evident by her asking how to do the activity of creating a Hawaii PowerPoint. How can a classroom in Manhattan and one in the South Bronx two years earlier be the same and different? In her writing, Lobman refers to what my students and I are doing as an improvisational performance or unscripted learning. According to her we are creating

> ...the supportive and creative learning environment where everyone can contribute what they can in order to help everyone learn (Lobman & Lundquist, 2007, p. 4).

The activity of creating a supportive and creative learning environment resolves the contradiction. The learning environment in the South Bronx produced engaging, organized activity that included "off task" activities. The "off task" activity was not related to as a problem, it was the improvisational "offer" that students were making. In many instances what they were doing was offering to play. Their ensemble performance produced the postures and gestures that I eventually learned to associate with a positive collaborative working environment where "rigorous project work" was happening in Manhattan. Within the context of all that "off task" activity in the South Bronx we were able to approach and engage a student in creating a project that was of interest to her. It was a very small but significant step for that student, in particular, and for that group of students in general. During that class there was no evidence of the anger and hostility that was typical of that group. Lobman and other observers have identified high levels of engagement, collaboration and positive emotions in my classroom and that leads me to believe that Jim's Tech Class seems to be a desirable learning environment, a place where learning is possible, no matter where it happens.

Playing Around with PowerPoint

Depending on where they are coming from students will have varying degrees of familiarity with computer technology and software applications. My first project with students typically involves organizing them into pairs to produce a 10-slide Microsoft PowerPoint presentation. Why Microsoft PowerPoint? This was the software that was installed on New York City Department of Education computers during the time I was teaching in New York City public schools. It could have been Impress from OpenOffice.org or Keynote from Apple. At the time I knew that there was a good chance that many of the students had prior exposure to computers with Microsoft Windows and Microsoft PowerPoint. When I paired them up I made sure that at least one student in each grouping felt very confident about his or her ability to use the computer and the software. I was interested in seeing what the students could produce and how they worked together in groups. Each group had to agree on a topic, find pictures and create a narrative that introduced the audience to the topic. I encouraged students to include colorful backgrounds, pictures, fancy slide transitions, sound effects and any other special effects that they could figure out how to use. I wanted creating a slide show to be a playful activity. I encouraged students to share technical know-how and to be creative.

Supporting students to play with technology is demanding because they expect me to know the answer or be able to figure out what to do when they get stuck. Their expectations are reasonable; they've been trained to rely on a teacher to provide the answer. Sometimes, I don't know the answer, or the correct series of steps to produce the desired text that bounces across the screen. If the situation permits, I will tell the student that I don't know the answer but that we can figure it out together. If the situation is too hectic, I will find some other resource, a more knowledgeable student, the Help text in the application, or an online website. When none of those resources are available, I encourage the student to keep playing around for a while longer and I offer suggestions on how to proceed such as, "try the animation button" or "don't spend too much more time on this, the priority is to get to ten slides." My goal is to simply keep the student from getting overly frustrated or bogged down with getting things right. I am always interested in engaging students when they struggle and learning about how they respond to the various types of help that are available or being offered.

Is it true that after more than 25 years of working with computers that a student could present me with a problem that I didn't know the answer to? Yes, in fact it happens all the time. The rate of technical change makes it impossible to keep up with everything that is new and available to students. What I am confident about is that whatever the problem is, we can find a way to move forward. In my initial interactions with students I want to show them that it is possible to move forward with a situation without knowing exactly how.

DEVELOPING A NEW APPROACH

In the narratives and vignettes I have tried to convey a sense of my experience in Jim's Tech Class and what happens there. Jim's Tech Class is the scene, a created learning environment, in which an ensemble performance is taking place. Certain elements of the scene are scripted and some are not, they are improvised. The scripted parts of the scene are easily recognizable and the roles and characters are familiar. There is a teacher, there are students and they are sitting in a classroom. The teacher is walking around making sure the students are "on task." The students are working and asking questions, there is a task that must be completed, etc. The improvisation is happening between the members of the ensemble. The interactions are both mundane and little surprising. Teachers don't normally admit to students that they "don't know" do they?

Why is the mini-lesson that includes a model of what students are supposed to do missing? How are students being assessed? What standards are being used? All of these questions point to the scripted part of the scene that was not featured in the narrative or the vignettes. Do these things happen in Jim's Tech Class? Yes, they have. My purpose here is to feature a performatory approach to pedagogy that can and does happen within the constraints and requirements of an ordinary school day while providing students with opportunities to use technology and creativity in their learning.

New Performances

The teacher is a performer and the students are performers. Teachers and students create scenes continuously and take turns being the audience and multiple foci in any learning scene. Raising a hand and answering a question would be a performance. Asking to go to the bathroom is another. Are these scripted or improvised? They are both. There are many happenings in the classroom that are predictable. Teachers and students are continuously anticipating certain responses to certain actions. They draw on their own histories in school and with each other to inform their performance in the current situation.

For example, Johnny always asks to go to the bathroom when the teacher begins the math lesson. The teacher is irritated with Johnny's pattern and responds to Johnny with a very angry tone of voice. All that Johnny has to do is raise his hand and the anger starts to well up inside the teacher as he anticipates the question and begins to experience resentment for the coming distraction from the lesson. The teacher is in a rut and his response is scripted and predictable. Everyone in the room knows what comes next. It is a script that plays out in schools everywhere. Can Johnny's teacher find an improvisational response or a new performance in responding to Johnny's bathroom request? Certainly, but the teacher has to be willing to do new things before he will be able to respond to Johnny improvisationally or with a new performance. He has to commit to saying "yes, and" to Johnny's request. He has to allow for the possibility of a new performance for himself and from Johnny even though he already knows what Johnny will say. By the way, Johnny is in a rut as well, he may be avoiding the bad feelings and frustration he experiences when a math lesson begins. Perhaps he would rather leave the room or get into an argument with the teacher than sit through a math lesson. Or maybe he has a problem managing his bladder because he always drinks water before math. The point is we don't know what kind of new performance is possible for Johnny or his teacher, but we know that one is possible if we allow them the space and provide support to create one. Johnny has just as much work ahead of him as his teacher does. Creating an environment for new performances is possible if we are willing to set aside our tendency to know what comes next in favor of more creative responses. This can happen while working with students to create opportunities to take responsibility and provide leadership and caring to a situation.

Emotions, Relationships, Responsibilities

Am I willing to examine my emotional reactions to what goes on around me and take responsibility for how I respond? Am I angry? How am I performing angry? Can I change my performance of being angry? During the writing of this book I read an article in the news about a teacher who was attacked by a student for not allowing him to go to the bathroom. The teacher claimed that she was instructed by the principal not to allow students to go to the bathroom during class time. How did following the principal's instructions impact on the teacher's and student's collective responsibility for what was happening between them? I don't know much more about that situation, but I can say with confidence that the environment where a creative solution could be generated did not exist for the people in that situation and they were angry about it. We have to take responsibility for creating creative learning environments even when unreasonable constraints are placed on us. We have to provide leadership to others when we recognize that we are getting angry about our circumstances. Looking at what is happening between people as if it were a theatrical performance is very useful when you are interested in creating change, or new performances. The use of improvisation's "yes, and" helps performers to break out of frustrating conversations that lead nowhere.

Director

In conversations I've had with educators about collaborative learning environments there is a tendency to identify a teacher's role as that of facilitator. The job of a facilitator is to make something easier, in this particular instance, the work of a group of students. I view my work as that of a director, I guide and I am in charge of the group's activity. As the director I try to create the most demanding environment possible, I try to minimize scripted interactions and I insist that students take responsibility for their choices. I see the role of director as taking responsibility for what is going on. I will even go as far as allowing students to direct me as a way being publicly accountable for my teaching practices.

Practice

Practice is where I generate my theories about what is going on in my classroom or the learning environment that I am creating with others. A theory about what is going on helps with generating questions. Why aren't they learning? Better yet, why are they learning? During my master's degree program many of my colleagues and I would groan when we were presented with theories. As novice teachers we had discovered that the theories were not helpful to us in our struggle to establish our ways of being in our schools and our teaching practices. The theories we were learning were disconnected from our experiences. They didn't make sense in the contexts we were working in and so we talked about them in grad school and in our papers and exams and then ignored them at work.

Many of the theories we were taught focused on how individual children learned. What I was struggling with as a new teacher was crowd control, or what we call classroom management. I was also struggling with who I was in my school and who administrators, peers and students expected me to be. More generally I was experiencing the culture shock of being in what I experienced to be a hostile environment where nothing seemed to make sense. What I needed were some theories for working with the groups of students I was working with. I needed to know how people learn in groups, and how social settings influence how people in groups learn. I needed a theory for how to perform in an unpredictable, emotionally charged environment with diverse children with diverse needs. Finally, I needed a theory for moving forward in the face of not understanding or knowing.

I was fortunate in that I had experienced a practice of creating learning environments or Vygotskian zones of proximal development (ZPD) (Vygotsky, 1978), prior to becoming a teacher. I recognized that I needed a safe environment to produce the conditions in which the theories (tools) would be relevant and I needed support so that I could learn from my experiences (successes and mistakes with students) and develop as a teacher. Like all too many teachers, what I needed to develop, as a teacher wasn't available to me in the school. I decided to go outside of the school for the support that I felt I needed. I had a vague sense that what I needed was out there and that what I needed to do was reach out for some help.

Groups and How I met Lev Vygotsky

Lev Vygotsky is often introduced to teachers in the context of social constructivist learning along with a brief description of what a ZPD is and a couple of paragraphs on "scaffolding" which is often and incorrectly in some texts attributed to Vygotsky (Holzman, 2009). In my grad school textbook he was introduced in the same chapter as Jean Piaget. My first contact with a Vygotskian learning environment was through participation in the youth development programs of the All Stars Project in New York City that used his notion of a ZPD in their after-school youth development programs.

I started volunteering in the All Star Project's Development School for Youth after-school program in 1996 where I taught high school students how to work in teams to do projects on computers. I did this with the direction and support of Pam Lewis, the program director. At the time, I was not a teacher and I had no experience in producing workshops with high school students. I was a volunteer and financial contributor to the All Stars Project. I learned that I was being related to as a learner who was being supported to do what he didn't know how to do by more experienced members of the organization. If I made mistakes, as I am sure I did, I couldn't exactly tell you what they were because no one ever told me that I "got it wrong." I always had the impression everyone I met at the All Stars Project was interested in helping me to increase my participation. The program staff and other volunteers always seemed eager provide more direction and support to what I was doing.

I kept getting invitations to attend events or to increase the amount of volunteering that I did. The thing that made it unusual was that I kept getting opportunities to do things that I wouldn't have selected for myself or felt I was qualified to do. I was getting opportunities to "perform a head taller." I learned that this was a phrase that Vygotsky used to describe when a learner was learning to do things that he could not yet do on his own. I learned how to do some of the things that were critical to the operations of a non-profit like making fund raising calls, hosting cocktail parties, and speaking in public about the organization. At the time, these were all very new activities for me. Yet, somehow, at All Stars Project events and performance spaces, I felt welcomed, safe and supported to take risks. Being treated so well by so many different people caused me to think that the attention was about me, but over time I observed that everyone was being related to in the way that I described. It wasn't about me; it was about creating the environment that I was participating in. There was a supportive quality to the environment that made it easier for me to do things that I had not imagined doing and that I didn't have an opportunity to do any place else.

The ZPD is considered one of Vygotsky's most important contributions. Two of the founders and builders of the All Stars Project over the past forty years, Lois Holzman and her intellectual collaborator Fred Newman, are scholars who have written many books and papers describing their use of Vygotsky's theories in their own practice of "developing a development community" and their unique approach to group therapy which they call social therapy. It was their work that I started reading as I became more involved in youth development and the type of learning that was going on in the youth programs of the All Stars Project. An example of a Vygotskian ZPD is that of a young child learning language in a family or community setting.

In a family or community setting experienced language speakers relate to a child as a speaker ahead of his or her ability to use language. The baby babbles and gestures and we say, "Oh, you want your bottle!" We use the inarticulate babble to create meaning, we are *making meaning with the baby* in the context of it's babbling or crying and our saying, "Oh, you want your bottle!" and presenting the bottle. After a certain amount of time and interaction the baby's babble starts sounding like the words we use for things when we are interacting with her. She will start to exert control over her environment through language; she is developing as a speaker and a learner. The baby's caregivers may be unaware that they are creating meaning and co-constructing an environment where many things can be learned as they interact with the baby.

In a ZPD more experienced members of a community or a group bring less experienced or new members along by interacting with them and involving them in whatever activity the community is engaged in. It would be unusual for someone to be concerned if a two year old could not identify a noun or a verb in her own speech. We don't teach language in the home by breaking down the components and memorizing the different categories of language. We learn language by participating in the activity of using language in the course of living. When the baby makes a mistake we don't chastise her for getting it wrong, we find a way to make sense of the interaction and move on, we trust that the baby will eventually say "bottle" instead of "bahbah."

ZPDs involve groups of people, not merely a teacher and a student interacting, but many diverse learners and experienced members of a community interacting. An astute student of mine once pointed out that a ZPD didn't seem to be of benefit to the "most experienced others" in the group. It was an excellent observation that was based in an understanding that presumes that "experienced others" gain little from their interactions "with less experienced others." The presumption that ZPDs are about "learning" flowing in one direction from the "more experienced" to the "less experienced" does not hold up if you consider the totality of what can be learned. Parents and caregivers recognize that they are learning many things in their interactions with children that go beyond the language activity that is occurring. In a ZPD new experiences and performances are being created for all participants and diversity is key in providing the greatest variety of experiences and the greatest opportunities to learn (Holzman, 2009). In the next section I share some thoughts about creating a performance of teaching out of what there is.

PERFORMING TEACHING

At a high school open house I attended with my daughter I heard a technology teacher say that she believed that she had the toughest job in her school because she couldn't teach students to use the tools (computers and software applications) outside of the context that what you would use them for in real life. I couldn't agree more. Other teachers that I have worked with have reported that they were teaching a technology class or the media studies class in addition to their own subjects because their schools had no one else. These teachers tended to be younger and/or "tech savvy" according to the administrators that handed out these assignments. While these teachers may have been "tech savvy" they may have also been at a loss to determine what the curriculum would be, how to deal with technology problems, and how to organize and assess student projects. Many of the experienced teachers I have known have been reluctant to disrupt the smooth and efficient flow of their teaching to integrate technology or a new methodology into their practice.

How do I incorporate a new technology or approach to my teaching? I try to see myself as a performer in a setting that is transforming and who can be changed, moved or influenced by the activity in which I am engaged in. The technology becomes another part of the scene that we are all interacting with. If it doesn't work, it's just another event in the scene that I or someone else must respond to, it's not a reflection on me. In other words, I allow the things that are happening around me to have an impact on what I do next.

I consider a new technology as something that might make a new performance possible. That performance might include finding new ways to communicate with students, parents, colleagues and administrators. The new technology might disrupt predictable and taken for granted routines. The new technology might present an opportunity to make the students (performers) look good in a way that was not previously possible. Students might recognize and be able to utilize the technology in ways that are creative and outside of my experience.

A new performance, such as using technology in the classroom, is a new development, you have learned to do something that you weren't previously capable of. Sometimes a new development is easy to perceive and sometimes it may be impossible to detect. Valuing the human capacity to perform and develop means that you are working to create environments where that is possible even if you can't measure it. I see the outcome of a developmental learning environment as being a social setting where human beings are engaged in diverse relationships, acknowledging emotionality, learning, and attempting to go beyond themselves.

Stage, Setting and Audience

I've heard many of my colleagues say that we have to create "stages for development" (Holzman, 2008). I've learned that we have to create a stage for development wherever we happen to be. If you are a teacher, there is the educational system you work in and all the policies, procedures and expectations that place demands on you and your students. Most of the time your students start out as strangers with unique histories, personalities and abilities who you will form relationships with over the course of a year. There is also your history, the subject that you teach, your skills, passions, interests, emotions and everything else that you are willing or able to bring to the learning environment. There is the community that supports your teaching and holds you accountable; this includes students, parents and other parties with interests in education at your school. There is the physical environment that you meet your students in, this includes the furniture, fixtures, the walls, roof, and space, or lack of it, and the technology that we use in everyday life in the context of this world at the particular historical moment you happen to be in. All of this and more, is what is available to us as we make choices about what we want to do with "what there is" and in particular, to create new learning environments with our students. Considering all that there is, it should not be surprising that trying to create change or something new in an institutional context is a daunting task.

Yes and

I use the language of theatre to help support and describe the new ways of being that are being presented here. As a performer I've learned to use improvisational techniques. For example, "yes, and" is a phrase used to indicate that I have accepted what is being offered. What I am suggesting here is that we accept "what there is" as an offer and work with others to create something new. In my experience, "yes, and" forces me to be more creative in responding to all kinds of situations. It allows me to be less defensive, less threatening, and positions me to provide a positive response to a negative situation. Saying "yes, and" or indicating agreement, is extremely hard when you are very stressed or very angry and extremely useful if you can actually do it in that type of situation. Finding the source of a disagreement, i.e. poor communications, an un-stated assumption, or lack of understanding is helpful, but creating agreement is how we can actually move forward in a situation. Developing the capacity to improvise and create agreement in the face of conflict and hostility requires the support of others. In other words, you have to *actively build the environment with others* for new performances and development to be possible. I've found that doing technology integration in school is a performance that is granted the space, support and flexibility needed to support change. As we go on this exploration together take the opportunity to examine your own practices and situation as a necessary part of being creative and critical in your effort to integrate technology into your teaching.

Performing and Technology Integration as Creating Change

Are learning to perform and use technology in the classroom worth the extra time and effort? As I mentioned in the first sentence in this book, it's about becoming a better teacher and no matter what route you take to that goal, it will take extra time and effort. It's been my experience that the majority of my students invest more time and energy in their technology integrated projects than I would ever ask or expect of them. Parents have told me on Parent-Teacher night that they believe that their kids are learning great things in the classroom and in the online environments that I have created. On the occasions when I have been able to work with teachers on integrating technology into their teaching practices I have used a performatory approach in creating the learning environment. On those occasions we have produced highly collaborative and engaging environments where students and teachers were taking risks, supporting each other, being creative and doing meaningful work that was rigorous and usually fun. I think it's been worth the extra effort and I am a rewarded by some of the positive changes in the lives of students and teachers I have worked with.

Continuous advances in technology make it possible to keep pushing the limits of what can be accomplished with technology. Teaching rubrics and standards must be updated to keep pace with students who are producing multimedia websites that feature the latest technologies and student created media artifacts. In this environment it is simply not possible for the knowledge acquisition model of learning (learning to acquire knowledge of facts) to remain the exclusive focus of the teaching practice. In fact, if we want to prepare students for a world in which the tools and media of work and civic engagement are constantly changing we also need an approach to developing student creativity, critical thinking and social responsibility. I am not suggesting that we can or should push the knowledge acquisition model of learning to the side to do other things. What I am suggesting is that as individual practitioners we have to become aware of the broader context in which we teach and take responsibility for restructuring what we teach given the constraints we operate within and the opportunities that are available. Reorienting the teaching practice to creating learning environments for groups of students and developing new methodological approaches to teaching is something that can be done, is inclusive of what we already do, and transforms what there is.

LET'S PAUSE HERE

Your circumstances influence or give shape to how you use the tools that are available. Writing the book has been useful to me in ways that I had not imagined, so I am reluctant to propose anything that might constrain you. However, I will offer some suggestions in the hopes that they will serve to prime your creativity or help you see your circumstances differently. At the end of each chapter I've provided some chapter highlights and some questions that can be used to initiate group discussion about themes related to the chapter. As you read, take an opportunity to share anything that surprises, confuses, provokes or challenges you in the text with a colleague. The progression in the book is not linear or chronological. My best suggestion is to use the book as a jump off point in your own exploration of new approaches to pedagogy and technology in the classroom. Write your own vignettes about what happens, share them with people, get feedback, reflect and then rewrite.

Have fun reading this book. Jim's Tech Class was a fun place to be, reading a book about Jim's Tech Class and creating learning environments should also be fun. When I run into a former student he or she always talks about how much fun it was, how students got to do whatever they wanted, and how easy it was. I used to get a bit worried when students said that my class was fun and easy. I was afraid that others (administrators) would get the impression that students weren't learning and that there was no academic rigor. My aim is to create an experience of reading this book that bears a resemblance to the type of fun learning that went on in my class. I eventually convinced myself that there was a great deal of rigorous learning activity in the learning environments we created and hopefully you will be able to use what is being offered here in your own teaching practice. One other thing, in order to learn about the work I am presenting, you actually have to do more than read. The fun and learning happen when you allow yourself to share, make mistakes, get help, try something new, collaborate, be surprised and get yourself engaged in a meaningful project. In the next chapter we meet a teacher in New Jersey and I provide an autobiographical account of the people and events that were significant in my development as an educator.

HIGHLIGHTS

– A vignette featuring Jim's Tech Class is provided as example of a technology rich learning environment in a middle school setting.
– Lev Vygotsky's zone of proximal development (ZPD) is introduced briefly and the author establishes his relationship to Vygotsky's work in settings that are outside of school.
– Ethnography is presented as a tool that was used in the development of the author's teaching practice as well as a tool for providing descriptions and accounts of experiences and events in different learning environments.
– An example is provided to describe a Vygotskian ZPD
– A conversation with a mentor over lunch leads to a reflection on the salient features of Jim's Tech Class by recalling an earlier episode in the teacher's career in the context of a recent observation.
– The thinking behind the use of PowerPoint presentations in the classroom as a first assignment is presented.

QUESTIONS FOR DISCUSSION

1. What does collaborative learning look like in your learning environment?
2. How would you describe your performance of being a teacher?
3. What are the challenges of working with diverse learners when introducing a new activity and how do you address those challenges?
4. How do you feel when confronted with a new challenge and what resources do you draw on for support?
5. What does knowledge acquisition learning look like in your learning environment and how does it compare to learning that takes place outside of school?
6. What is challenging or provocative about the author's stance on knowledge acquisition learning?

A HISTORY OF LEARNING IN AND OUT OF SCHOOL

Elementary Improv

If I could figure out a way to get paid for doing this in schools, life would just be great. That's what I thought as the 3rd grade public school kids hugged me and waved goodbye as they lined up to go to another classroom. I was visiting their classroom in Jersey City, New Jersey and we had just finished our first workshop together. I had introduced the idea of performance and playing improvisation games as part of a literacy unit that they were doing with their teacher. The technology component would include typing scripts on a computer and performing skits in front of a digital video camera. Some students are shy about video cameras and seeing themselves in a video, but in my experience many more are highly motivated by the idea of seeing themselves in video. The goal was to produce a DVD of the performances and to show the writing that was part of producing the performances on a Blog or Wiki. As the next group of 3rd graders came in for a half hour of literacy instruction, their teacher Ms. Rosario surprised me by asking me to do the workshop with the next group.

We hadn't planned on it but she was clearly excited about what had just gone on in her classroom and she wanted to see if we could have similar success with the next group. I was willing, so we organized the students on the reading rug and started introducing the idea that human beings are performers. The students were able to identify all sorts of performers and performances. All of the students seemed to participate in the ten-minute conversation. I invited them to play an improv game as a warm-up exercise. I explained that being able to play a game together meant that we could perform together and work together. All of the students participated, and like the first group, they enjoyed the game. They struggled with some aspects of the game even as they laughed and made mistakes. When we finished playing the game we had enough time do one improvised scene before their lunchtime bell rang. It was a lot of fun, even for the boy who admitted that he was scared. He was on our "pretend stage" with two girls who jumped right into the scene by asking in unison "What are you scared of?" The young fellow looked at me confused and said "I didn't know we were starting." I said, "that's okay, you are on stage and we are going to use what you said." He remembered that the scene was set in a forest and said timidly, "the animals." The threesome continued the scene for a few more seconds, generating laughter all around and I choose that moment to end the scene by clapping and praising a great performance. As this group of students left the class they also asked about when we would do this again.

When Ms. Rosario called me later that evening she expressed her thanks and a great deal of enthusiasm. She said that the students had started talking about what they had done in the lunchroom with their peers. Ms. Rosario had also started talking to her peers and had mentioned the project to an art teacher who offered his time and resources to help with making props for the scenes that students would write. She also told me about one girl who really surprised her, she said that this girl never raised her hand or participated in classroom discussions but she had done so on this occasion. I was happy that everyone was so excited and I told Ms. Rosario I was looking forward to my next visit and that we would talk soon to plan what we would do next.

In this the rest of this chapter I will fill in some of the blanks on how I got to be the guy who walks into a classroom and gets students and teachers so excited to be at school.

New York Puerto Ricans

My father came to the United States from Puerto Rico at the age of thirteen, on a cargo plane that lost a door in mid-flight in the 1950s. My mother came as a child in the late 1930s, on an ocean freighter, and remembers eating nothing but apples for several for days. Both of my parents lost their mothers in childhood and were separated from their fathers, until their families were reconstituted in the United States in New York City. My grandparents were born before Puerto Ricans became citizens of the United States in 1917. The Spanish had ruled Puerto Rico since 1492 and colonized Puerto Rico with Spanish culture for about 400 years. The Catholic Church had arrived with the Spaniards and played a key role in the colonization of Puerto Rico and the education of its people and so my parents and grandparents were Catholic and spoke Spanish. The connections to the indigenous Taino culture of the island were severed during the process of colonization. Spain had undertaken the process of granting Puerto Ricans autonomy when the Spanish American War in 1898 cut the process short. When my mother describes the history of my family there are many grafts (step-parents, common law spouses, adopted children) in the family tree, and the documented history doesn't go back beyond my much further than great grand parents on either side of the family. She also says that there aren't many relatives who tell stories about the past in the family; it seems to me that there were a lot of things that my relatives would rather forget.

New York City Boy

I was raised in New York City. The migratory experiences of my family are common for Puerto Ricans and my own ambiguity around the idea of a central or a fixed cultural identity is consistent with what Juan Gonzales (2000) describes as a "profoundly schizophrenic migrant experience" and is summarized with the following: "The contradiction of being at once citizens and foreigners, when joined with the reality that ours is a racially mixed population…" I've had more than a few people ask me what I was. More often than not they are surprised to learn that I am Puerto Rican, sometimes I can see that the surprise is pleasant for them, their families are also from some place else and they identify with me. Other people don't know what a Puerto Rican is and I have to explain that I am an American citizen.

I discovered that students have stereotypes about Puerto Ricans and they are sometimes surprised by the contradictions I raise for them. They ask questions like, "How can you be a teacher?" "How come you don't have an accent?" "Are you poor?" There have been several students who refused to believe that I was ever poor and that I grew up in dangerous public housing projects in New York City. I remember that while I was growing up I didn't want to be poor or identified as being brown or different. I was open to other influences, such as getting an education and planning on the type of job or career that would result in a high income. I had middle class ambitions.

Education in New York City

As I remember my career as a New York City public school student the negative experiences seem to outweigh the benign and/or positive experiences. It would be insincere of me to even attempt a balanced perspective from my own accounts. However, I will share some vivid memories that fuel my bias and are still what I believe are common experiences for students four decades later. Then, I will reflect on the outside of school experiences that offered models of learning and leadership that were alternatives to the learning opportunities that I received in public school.

I started attending school in 1968, when I was five years old. I was in a Head Start program and I don't remember much except that it seemed fun until the day I met my first bully. He and his friend forced my playmate and I off the Seesaw by threatening to hit us. It was the first time I can recall being afraid of another child. Later on, in the 4th grade I was placed into what progressive educators at the time called an Open Classroom. I don't remember what I learned except that I was afraid of reading aloud. I was so nervous I stuttered when I read, and I couldn't do the math very well. We rotated to different work areas all day and I remember that there were children who teased or made fun of me on a regular basis when we worked independently. I felt I was somehow different but I didn't know how. I wasn't the smallest kid in the room, I was somewhere in the middle of the height ordered line, I had thick dark hair parted to the side, and my olive colored skin tanned brown easily. I thought I looked like an ordinary kid, just like all the others.

Over time the bullying started to escalate from teasing and name-calling to physical conflicts and it seemed to me that everyone (a few of the boys and some of the girls) picked on me. My elementary school, PS 145, was located on the Upper West Side of Manhattan and was economically and culturally diverse. My classmates were Puerto Rican, Dominican, White, Black, and Chinese. I had the same teacher and classmates from 4th through 6th grade. I was aware that the teacher was including me in the "smart groups," but to me the White kids in those groups were always smarter than I was. When I compared my grades with others I was somewhere in the middle of the pack rarely the highest never the lowest. I remember going to different specialized schools to take admission tests in the 6th grade. I never did well enough to be accepted into any of those schools so I went to the neighborhood junior high school.

Junior high school was an absolutely miserable experience for me. I was placed into the Special Progress class because I was considered smart. The White kids had all gone to other schools so now I was at the top of the class. The only people I knew in junior high school were the Latino kids who had been at my elementary school. Schoolwork never seemed to be much of a problem, but there were many fights with other students, these seemed to be a continuation of the bullying that had started in elementary school some of the same people were involved. The violence was now occurring in the classroom during lessons, not just during independent work time, or in the hallways, or at gym. I dreaded going to school and avoided being there during lunch (we were able to go home for lunch) and I never attended school-based after-school programs. I knew that the people who bullied me attended after-school programs. Despite my efforts to avoid being noticed the bullies seemed to find me.

The teachers spent a lot of time scolding and yelling at us. I was frequently bored. I wasn't a talented athlete and I felt uncomfortable in social situations, I had more in common with the "uncool" kids than the cool ones. My clothes were never in style and I wore them until they could no longer be worn. I spent my time reading science fiction and comic books, playing baseball in the park, and going to church with my family. We didn't travel on vacations and we didn't have a lot of acquaintances to visit with, my world was north of 96th street and south of 125th street and between the Hudson River and Central Park.

Religious Instruction

Sister Maria Magdalena was the Catholic nun who ran Sunday school, the summer day camp and after-school religious instruction. She was probably involved in many other things that I was not aware of. She organized the primarily Latino parents on the Upper West Side of Manhattan during the 60s and 70s. One of the striking things about Sister Maria was that she very petite and seemed to be in charge of everything. On Sundays Sister Maria ran the Sunday school and provided religious instruction in English and in Spanish to parents after Sunday mass while the children attended an hour of Sunday school. She trained parents and teenagers to run Sunday school classes for the community. As a teenager I took my turn teaching Sunday school, tutoring in the after-school program in the church basement, working as a summer day camp counselor and doing anything else that Sister Maria told or asked me to do. There was a different community of kids at the church and none of the neighborhood bullies were part of that community.

I recall the image of a petite Sister Maria standing in the middle of a group of towering teenage boys and commanding and directing them to carry out the day's tasks. It's strange but I do not remember even one instance where someone disrespected Sister Maria. That, somehow, did not even seem to be a remote possibility, as if the idea had never occurred to anyone. I don't recall being afraid of Sister Maria, and I didn't always want to do what she told me to do, but for some reason I did it anyway. Unlike the stereotype for nuns she did not have a reputation for punishing children with a ruler. She rarely needed to scold anyone.

Looking back, maybe her institutional location as a nun, plus the practical experience of her as a teacher and community leader and had something to do with all the respect she got. She had what very few adults have in everyday life. She embodied multiple aspects of institutional authority while at the same time generating authority from many relationships with parents in the community and young people of all ages. There were so many people going along with what Sister Maria was doing in the community that objecting to helping to decorate the church for Christmas or not showing up to bible study would have seemed out of the ordinary. The ordinary things that Sister Maria asked us to do, I think, were part of why it all worked. Ordinary people did all the things that were positive and supportive in the community and those things didn't require extraordinary effort or resources, they were easy to do. Sister Maria kept us involved in our own community and through that involvement we learned, developed and were given responsibilities that were important to the community.

Community of Practice

Jean Lave and Etienne Wenger are researchers that describe this type of learning environment as legitimate peripheral participation in a community of practice (Lave & Wenger, 1991). The new comers in the community, in this case children, are brought in to the community of practice (being part of the community that attends a Catholic church) by adults and more experienced peers through a gradual process of participation in activities that require increased skill and knowledge that are acquired through increased interactions with skilled practitioners. As the new comers become old timers (children become adolescents who teach Sunday school) they take responsibility for the participation of new comers and become active in perpetuating the community of practice. The community of practice (the Church community) is a particular social setting and members within the group have different levels of ability and resources within the setting of that practice.

The performatory features of this type of learning environment are apparent from my point of view. Children perform being Sunday school students and then later as adolescents, they perform as Sunday school teachers. The members of the community support the young people by relating to them as Sunday school teachers before they are actually experienced teachers. This learning environment features young people having responsibility for something that is important to the community (teaching Sunday school) and adults providing the support (mentoring, resources, opportunities, etc.). Lois Holzman and Fred Newman are scholars and community builders who have discovered, that through performance human beings in groups are capable of learning to do new things, before they actually *know* how to do them and that this is developmental (Newman & Holzman, 1997).

Marital Arts Practice

One summer when I was about fourteen a Black man came to our summer day camp and demonstrated a martial art called Wing Chun Kung Fu. He invited the teenagers to take classes that would be held at the neighborhood health clinic where he worked as an X-ray technician. Each class was only $2.00 for each person so some of us decided to check the classes out. That was the start of my martial arts training and I would continue that training until I was about nineteen. My training included many hours of practice and many conversations with Sifu (this is how we referred to our teacher) and my Wing Chun brothers and sisters about technique and practical applications. We were always eager for more techniques, we were always eager to learn.

At first Sifu would lead the class and we always followed the same warm up routine. After the first year he would occasionally arrive late (because we moved to a different location) and would have one of us lead the routine while he changed into his workout clothes. After awhile we just started running class (we often arrived early) and practicing our drills so that when Sifu arrived he wouldn't have to spend time getting us ready to practice with him. Practicing with Sifu was the highlight of class for each student, he would correct posture, hand positions, and would remind us to breath through our noses. While Sifu worked with individuals, other students paired up and practiced the newest techniques in our increasing inventory of skills. We found that even the most basic techniques could become interesting in new ways as we became more experienced and began to see the basics as a foundation for more complex situations. Practice was fun and those of us who were committed always showed up early and stayed late.

The interaction of the group was central to our skills development. Sifu would promote us as a cohort, which meant that we all got a new technique at the same time. What seemed important was that we worked together to master our techniques. Sifu said it would make no sense to promote a student on his own without insuring that he had others to practice with. According to Sifu our diversity in size, strength, speed, etc. was of value to our practice, it was value that each of us could bring and benefit from. When I was among the other students in the class I never experienced any fear or the anxiety that I had when I was in school. Teasing and joking was good-natured, we experienced high levels of camaraderie. Looking back, we were kind of like a gang, we supported each other, there was a clear leader, we understood our ranking relative to each other, and we understood that there was a process to membership in the group.

My relationship to bullies and fighting also changed. I came to know what I could do in a fight. Sifu always advised us to avoid fights at all costs. True mastery was about avoiding creating the kinds of environments that produced fights. He also understood that there would be times when a fight was unavoidable. He instructed us to operate under the assumption that the opponent was armed and that a fight would result in at least one party going to the hospital. He elevated the idea of a fight to being an activity with grave consequences that required commitment and responsibility. Upon reflection and looking at it as a performance, he transformed a fight for me from something that little boys do in the hallway to something that young men did as a last resort. Somehow, bullying and name-calling weren't worth worrying about. By the time I was sixteen we had added new students to our little school and the original students were given the task of providing foundational training to the newer students, which included other teens and adults. Sifu explained it was important for us to understand that the newer students would never have the same access to him that we had. Our taking responsibility for the newer students allowed him to continue to focus on our instruction while at the same time expanding the size of the school and developing his own practice. The school was a hierarchy with membership based on skills and commitment. Our participation in training newer students would also develop our teaching skills and prepare us to be teachers in our own schools

Sifu was in his early thirties when he began teaching us and he was still attending classes with his own teacher and peers. Although I didn't recognize it at the time, he was a grassroots organizer and a Black leader who was doing positive things for inner city kids. What he accomplished in the late 1970s and early 1980s would not be possible thirty years later. He operated without insurance, and without a permanent location and no funding. He worked with churches and other community institutions to acquire free space for us to practice. The $2.00 fee was symbolic, our demonstration that the training was worth an economic commitment on our parts. Our parents never questioned his credentials and never came to our practices. My parents knew some of the other boys in class, they knew where to find us, and they believed in safety in numbers. We, together with Sifu, made our school possible. It was a great learning experience. As we grew up and the circumstances of our lives changed, our school eventually ended. We all moved on, changed by the experience.

As I reflect back on these early learning experiences I notice that there are some striking similarities between the learning environment at church and in Kung Fu class. Both environments required the learner to choose among opportunities being offered and make commitments that went beyond merely showing up, committed participation was required. There was an expectation that new members in the learning environment would be brought along not only by the leaders but by more experienced peers. Learning, as a member of the community happened as new roles and responsibilities were taken on and development happened over time as existing relationships to other members, knowledge, skills and circumstances changed. These environments were also top-down oriented and fairly inflexible, the learner had very little to offer with respect to new knowledge or outside interests other than his or her willingness to provide a source of labor in the prescribed manner.

The Purpose of Education

In my family, the role of the first-born son was to work hard, set a good example, go to college, get a good job and make a decent living. I went to a large vocational high school that selected students through a competitive process, the problem of physical bullying disappeared and in a culturally and economically diverse high school I could blend into the crowd. Nonetheless even in high school, I experienced more subtle forms of bullying such as being called a "brainiac" or a "know it all" when I emerged as a top student in biology and other classes. I didn't mind high school too much; I was travelling on my own in New York City on the subways. I participated in high school sports, and I did what I needed to do academically.

I did fairly well on the scholastic aptitude test, I even received a small New York State scholarship, but no one in my family had ever been to college and I didn't think I was smart enough to go to a big name Ivy League college. I applied to Hunter College, which is a local city college in Manhattan, it was a short bus or train ride away from home and I learned that I could get financial aid that would pay for it all. Hunter College turned out to be a pretty big and intimidating place, I didn't have anyone advising me so I took classes that were too difficult for a freshman to handle and I wound up failing a couple of courses like biology and chemistry. I didn't understand that I could withdraw from courses if I saw that I was in danger of failing. My grade point average was very low my first couple of years of college. Somewhere in my second or third year of college I declared economics as my major, I had no idea of what I was doing. I had been demoralized by my college performance in the sciences, which had been my interest in high school. My advisor at the time suggested that I take a couple of computer courses, I had been turned off to computers in high school and so I had no interest, but I enrolled in a course and got hooked on using IBM PCs. After a great deal of hard work and fun doing it, I figured out that computers were for me and that they could be my ticket to employment and a high income. I switched my major to computer science. I soon found myself to be the only Puerto Rican taking advanced computer science classes with students who were White, Asian and European. After five years of college I finally got out with a bachelor's degree in computer science.

My original interest in going to college was to have a career in the biological sciences. It was what I thought I was good at. Unlike the other activities that I had become good at, such as martial arts, or being involved at church, I had no community or group support for trying to get into a big school or doing science (biology, chemistry). There were no opportunities to take risks without serious consequences and there were no institutions or individuals that were visible to me to provide access to the necessary resources. That changed for me as a computer science major, there was a little community of students that hung out in the computer lab and professors often had favorite students that they encouraged and recommended for part-time programming and technical support jobs. I started earning money with tutoring and part time jobs hooking up computers in college, that was the beginning of my technology career.

Learning on Wall Street

I got to Wall Street and I stayed there for the better part of two decades. I never really considered the educational background of all the people who were influential in my professional development. Looking back now, I can appreciate that I was trained to work and think by pioneers of the information age. My mentors include two managers who were MIT graduates, and managers who had worked on the first computer systems ever built in the banking, airlines and telecommunications industries. I also had a network of peers that I could call upon to help me when I got stuck. We used technical jargon to create and participate in a culture that valued helping and collaboration. For me, having a good reputation and good relationships in the corporate technology community was a significant motivation for helping others.

In the corporate environment I learned to make phone calls, use corporate resources, participate in meetings, produce status reports, manage projects and interact with vendors. Work was fun, getting new computer equipment was like having Christmas everyday. Putting it all together and making it all work was like playing with toys and solving puzzles. I learned to perform the practical business skills that were required to operate in the global economy. I learned a White middle class performance in corporate America. I was fortunate that my corporate mentors, most of them anyway, were very generous and forgiving of my many early missteps. My career as a corporate technologist led me to consulting and eventually to the Dot-com 1990s where my entrepreneurial bubble expanded and popped. Along the way I started a family, had a nice salary, bought a brownstone in New Jersey, and became interested in learning and human development.

I learned that in the corporate world, education is a commodity that you trade on. It is about acquisition of skills and knowledge for the purpose of solving business problems or gaining competitive advantage. It was also about the school you came from, the degree you had and the social network you were a part of. My training as a programmer had prepared me for being a valuable commodity, but I was still socially and emotionally underdeveloped and I had not become part of an alumni network. As materially successful as I was becoming, I still had fear and anxiety about being smart enough and my relationship network was not deep or varied. As I got older my anxieties increased, work stopped being fun and the requirements of what would be called, "life long learning in the service of industrial-consumer paradigm" by one of my professors, Joel Spring (2006) had become both tedious and unrewarding. In the globalized corporation the skill and experience of individuals were separated from their value to the community and were not afforded the same status as in the Chinese martial arts, or in the community building activities that I had experienced in my youth. What people "know" and "do" in the global economy is considered a commodity to be purchased at the lowest price. The process for how we get to "know" and "do" and "become" as individuals in the context of a community of practice is de-valued. I was getting tired of being a commodity with declining value.

All Stars Project

A door knock, a door opening, and a donation; I entered the world of grassroots community organizing in an effort to help inner city kids to grow and develop by performing. The door knock came from a volunteer fundraiser going door to door in my neighborhood. She was raising money for an organization that is currently known as the All Stars Project. I believe that my generosity in that particular moment came from several places, I was a new parent and the baby had just started sleeping through the night, it was a gorgeous Saturday morning in the early spring, I had a few dollars in my pocket, I owned my home, and I had a very nice income. The volunteer had a nice pitch and helping inner city kids sounded like a good thing. I gave the contents of my pocket and didn't think about it again until the phone calls started a couple weeks later. The volunteers of the All Stars Project have a wonderful way of talking to people about their work and working with potential donors to say, "yes" to making contributions.

After several contributions and about a year later and I met Dr. Lenora Fulani one of the program's founders and the first Black woman to be on the ballot for President of the United States in all 50 states during 1988 election (yes, really, it's true, she just wasn't a "major party candidate"). She invited me to a meeting of financial contributors who were volunteering to be "teachers who weren't really teachers" at something she called the Development School for Youth (DSY), a 12-week after-school leadership program where we would teach inner city high school students leadership skills. Over the next seven years, while I was busy with my corporate consulting career, I volunteered at the DSY. Although I didn't know it at the time, I was learning to teach workshops using a Vygotskian, performatory social therapeutic approach to human development (Newman and Holzman, 1997). I also learned to fund raise, talk to strangers about the programs, work with young people, and build community. I was eventually asked to join the Board of Directors of the All Stars Project.

Fulani trained all of the adults who participated in working with the high school students in the DSY. Her training was intense and brought to the forefront the race and class issues that we adults brought to the program as well as what our responsibilities were in engaging the race and class issues that our students would bring. The training seemed very therapeutic. The emotions that were a result of and generated by what we were engaging seemed to be vital to Fulani's pedagogy. Some of the adults who I became friendly with reported emotional growth and development and I experienced that as well. We had gone into the program believing that we were teaching kids. What we discovered was that the activity of teaching the kids and being supported to "do what we did not already know how to do" (run workshops for high school students) provided us with opportunities to grow and develop socially and emotionally. Fulani also engaged our notions of what we thought we were teaching, and challenged our assumptions about how and why students of color failed in New York City public schools.

Most of us were successful experienced business people without credentials in education and we held common beliefs that education was focused on the wrong things. We had a variety of ideas about what students should know. Fulani challenged our notions of education for the purpose of "knowing" and "getting a job" and directed our attention to the activity of helping students develop new performances. These new performances would be the tools that our students would need to help them in the corporate internships that we would set up for them. What was required was that we help the students to perform without "knowing" and relate to them not as who they were, but as the young professionals they were in the process of becoming. We had to relate to them as "a head taller" a phrase that I came to recognize as a Vygotskian description of a learner who is being supported to perform beyond his current level of development. Performing in the corporate setting meant exposing the students to the culture, the skills, and the habits of the White middle class professional settings that we would support them in.

We taught the students how to shake hands, dress, interview, use computers, take cues from the people around them, and reach out for help when they were unsure. We created and directed these performances together, sometimes on a stage, sometimes in a mock interview at an office. The students didn't have to know particular things, they needed to perform in particular ways with others and as they performed they would gain knowledge during the course of their social interactions. Many of our students had, as I had realized about myself, stopped developing. The capacity to develop had to be re-initiated. Our method for doing so was to view hand shaking and interviewing as a performance that could be improved on with direction from more skilled performers in an environment where taking risks was supported and making mistakes was part of the development of a new performance. Fulani led and directed us in our new performances and in turn we led and directed the students.

I did not realize it at the time but this performatory social therapeutic approach to learning and developing in a group had qualities of best learning environments I had experienced. It is not surprising that the theories and practices of this new community resonated with me. The major difference was that this new learning environment was described as "bottom up" or "grassroots" and the learner was asked to offer more than labor.

A Teaching Fellow

My entrepreneurial venture failed late in 2000 and I was able to find a short consulting contract early in 2001. After September 11th of that year the technology sector job market in New York City, which had been bad, got worse. I didn't want a job that required 80% travel and I was trying to get out of the technology job treadmill that I felt I was on. Hundreds of resumes and job applications later, I happened to come across an advertisement for the New York City Teaching Fellows. I knew that I liked kids and I thought teaching would be a good thing to do and I could get a free master's degree. I could use all the things I learned at the All Stars Project and if teaching didn't work out then I could go back to a technology career when the market rebounded, so I applied and I was accepted.

I wound up teaching elementary school in the South Bronx and very quickly experienced teacher burnout. Breaking up fights among elementary school children was a daily event. I regularly came home with the stink of the perspiration that occurs when you are highly stressed. I worked in a school where the emergency services unit was parked outside on a weekly basis and the police escorted children out of the building in restraints. There were three fires during my first year in the school building.

My alarm was set at 5:30 AM and every morning it required an act of extreme effort to get up and go to work. Sunday night was the worst night of the week, I stressed over being prepared for the week and not wanting to go to work the next day. In the winter I prayed for snow days and I learned to count down the number of days left in the school year. The general environment in the South Bronx neighborhood I was working in was clearly impacting on me in negative ways. The neighborhood was desolate, there was always conflict on the buses and the trains, and people spoke to each other harshly in an almost casual manner. Displaying anger was a norm and I regularly caught myself becoming verbally abusive to others and I didn't treat myself very well either. The stress was literally killing me. I was turning forty and my hair was falling out and a variety of other physical problems were emerging. I knew during that time that I needed more support than what was being provided by the school system. Despite all of that, somewhere along the way, even with all the bad things that were happening to me, I had decided that being an educator was worth doing as a career. It was crazy.

Walls Without a University

The East Side Institute (the Institute) is an international training and research center for new approaches to human development and community building. I turned to the Institute during my first year of teaching in the South Bronx when I realized that teaching there was having a negative impact on my relationships and my health. I started attending workshops there that involved learning to use improvisation in the classroom. I started working with Lois Holzman and Carrie Lobman, her colleague at the Institute who was also a professor of early childhood education at Rutgers University. In working with Holzman and Lobman, I learned more about Vygotsky and the performatory approach to learning that was employed in the environments that I had volunteered in. I learned why I could not simply recreate these environments in public school settings. I had to create learning environments with what there was and I had to develop my capacity to perform and work with others.

In working with faculty at the Institute I discovered that there were different ways that I could build my relationships to students and improvise in and around the constraints imposed by the educational system. I could perform as a different kind of teacher and I could use theatrical improvisation to help my students in many small ways. I began to see my students as groups of learners and I began to understand that my job was to organize the groups and to create collaborative learning environments that featured students taking responsibility for their learning. I also had to take responsibility for my teaching by making what I was doing more public and transparent. Teaching with the door closed was no longer an option.

Holzman and Lobman helped me through my first three years of teaching and they designed a new program at the Institute, the Developing Teachers Fellowship Program, based on their work with teachers like me. After taking all the workshops that the Institute offered more than once, I found that I needed a more challenging activity to keep pushing myself to develop my teaching practice. I eventually began to volunteer with the Developing Teachers program and Holzman offered me an independent course of study at the Institute. We talked about my teaching practice and I did some research with her support and direction. She directed me to the work of Michael Cole who she had studied with at Rockefeller University and had introduced her to the work of Lev Vygotsky. She, like Fulani, was also a grassroots organizer with an expertise in human development, educational studies and community services. Holzman was the director of the Institute, which her collaborator Fred Newman often referred to as the "walls without the University."

Holzman related to me as a peer during our work together and I enjoyed the scholarly activity. From my experiences I concluded that public schools did not prioritize the development of scholarship and intellectual curiosity in teachers for the purpose of creating positive change in the world and I found that deeply frustrating. I realized that I couldn't remain in education if I could not work with people who were willing to work on changing the way things were. Shortly after the independent study, I decided to enter graduate school and get a Ph.D. I decided I would need official credentials to do the things that I was interested in doing in education. I need to create social capital that I lacked since I no longer had the trappings of a nice income and a corporate location at a Wall Street firm.

I credit the Institute for the fact that I remained in public schools for seven years. Teacher retention is a huge problem in hard to staff urban schools and many of the Teaching Fellows that I knew were out of New York City public schools in three years or less. Some of my peers who remained in teaching went into administration, private schools, and alternate educational settings or moved to suburban schools. I continued teaching in New York City throughout my doctoral program and ended my employment at the Department of Education after I graduated.

THE SEARCH FOR METHOD

The search for method becomes one of the most important problems of the entire enterprise of understanding the uniquely human forms of psychological activity. In this case, the method is simultaneously pre-requisite and product, the tool and result of the study. (Vygotsky, 1978, p 65)

In Holzman's many books, talks and workshops, she refers to Vygotsky's "search for method." She talks about his search for a new psychology, a new method for studying human beings that would help people during the revolutionary times that he lived and worked in (Holzman, 2009). In her own book Holzman describes her search for method and in my "creative imitation" of Holzman, this book is part of my "search for method," my scientific study of my teaching practice in its historical context using Vygotskian performatory social therapeutic approaches to creating learning environments.

The theories of learning and human psychology that are derived from Vygotsky's works are known as cultural-historical activity theory (CHAT), socio-cultural theory or Activity theory. These theories all reference and build on Vygotsky's contributions to psychology and education. Activity theorists and Vygotsky scholars are not unified in their understandings of Vygotsky or in the ways they have built upon his work, according to Holzman (2006) they are unified in their diverse perspectives.

Since we are not unified in perspective, I'd like to be clear on what our perspective is with respect to our ideas on method and conceptual tools. I have summarized some points from a training presentation (Holzman, 2011) given by Holzman to the teaching faculty at the East Side Institute where she is the director.

– Vygotsky's "search for method" is a new way of looking at method; method is an activity to be practiced, as opposed to being applied.
– Play is developmental activity that is associated with performance, and creative imitation. In play there is an opportunity to "be a head taller" as development happens.
– Development is accomplished in groups and communities; learning and development form a dialectical unity, and cannot be considered in isolation of each other.
– The zone of proximal development is not a space it is an activity.
– Learning is simultaneously creating the ZPD and the result of creating the ZPD with others who may be at different levels or may not have knowledge or tools but are accepted as co-creators in the activity anyway.
– We are born into culture and we are the creators of culture.
– Learning and development, play, performance, creating culture and the "search for method" are all "tool and result" types of activities that are considered to be dialectical unities or totalities. The results of these activities are not separate from the activities themselves.

The presentation also included the following quote, which is helpful in clarifying some of the bullet points.

> Every function in the child's cultural development appears twice: first on the social level, and later, on the individual level; first, between people *(interpsychological)*, and then *inside* the child *(intrapsychological)*. This applies equally to voluntary attention, to logical memory, and to the formation of concepts. All the higher functions originate as actual relations between human individuals. (Vygotsky, 1978 p. 57)

Development is something that happens between individuals first and so when we consider what the unit of interest should be in a learning environment, it should be the group. From the quote we see that the history of the higher functions is traced back to the cultural setting that development happened in. The acquisition of skills and knowledge using this framework is not accomplished through direct transfer from the more experienced to the less experienced individuals, but through the availability of skills and experience in the ZPD that is made possible through the joint-activity that individuals are participating in. When I refer to teaching students how to use technology I am referring to the activity that we are engaged in where it is possible for them to acquire skills and knowledge. My presence supplies a particular expertise that I can bring to the learning situation. In the course of our interactions or joint-activity I relate to them ahead of their current level of development. This is a departure from standard teaching practices. In this environment it is also possible for students to discover that they also have something to bring to the learning environment. As students contribute to the learning environment I have discovered that they unknowingly create an environment that is rich, complex and interesting enough to provoke me to push harder to create my own learning and development as I work with them to create theirs.

These are the tools of the qualitative inquiry that I am engaged in. Throughout my practice during the timeframe depicted in this book and during the development of the book I've tried to be consistent in my use of these tools even as my understanding of them developed. My effort here is like exploring off the clearly marked hiking trail, it's been hard work but I think there's a chance of finding something new and making a valuable contribution to the community.

HIGHLIGHTS

- The author provides examples from his own life experience to illustrate learning in groups in outside of school settings.
- Lave and Wenger's theory of communities of practice are used as a lens to view the learning of cultural practices such as participating in Kung Fu classes and Catholic church activities.
- The author provides his connection to Vygotsky, Holzman and Newman as he traces his historical development as a teacher.
- Bullying is prominent in the author's recollections of his formal schooling experience.
- Improvisation in a 3rd grade classroom is described as an intervention for creating new performances and new levels of enthusiasm in the classroom.
- Improvisation and performance are discussed in the context of the All Stars Project after-school programs.
- The author's own diversity and the diversity of the leaders and the social scenes he describes are evident throughout the chapter.
- Alternative social settings for students to have opportunities to develop and learn outside of school are presented.
- The author identifies his tools in his "search for method."

QUESTIONS FOR DISCUSSION

1. Can you describe the features of the best learning environments you've been a part of?
2. How does your history influence how you think about education or technology?
3. Can you describe a situation in which events led to a confrontation? Was the situation avoidable?

4. What do you mean when you use the word "diversity?"
5. What are the situations that you feel that you perform well in?
6. What are your interests and passions and are they served in school settings?
7. What kinds of challenges does bullying present?
8. Apart from what you read in this chapter, what do you know about Vygotsky?

THE "PROBLEM" IN EDUCATION

A key interest in integrating technology into learning environments is to create highly engaging learning experiences. In this chapter we look into Ms. Rosario's 3rd grade classroom to explore what an engaging and highly integrated technology classroom looks like. Despite her obvious success with technology and creating engaging lessons Ms. Rosario still experiences the problems that many other teachers experience. Highly engaging learning experiences don't seem to make certain problems go away.

What a Good Learning Environment Looks Like

Ms. Rosario, an early career 3rd grade teacher, expressed the following to me; "How do we even know what a good learning environment looks like? My principal says that a good learning environment looks like chaos, but when he looks into my classroom he only compliments us when the kids are sitting quietly at their desks writing." I had been working with Ms. Rosario's class for several weeks and I knew exactly what she was talking about. Every time I visited her classroom her 3rd graders were noisy, up out of their seats and engaged in various activities. I didn't make the environment any quieter, the students had learned to take my presence as a cue that they would start playing performance games, work on computers, use microphones, read and revise scripts and video record performances of those scripts.

Ms. Rosario's question indicated to me that on some level there was a shared understanding that good learning environments have chaotic features and that there was a contradiction, quiet reading and writing was the activity that was praised. Ms. Rosario was worried that the chaos would be interpreted as a situation that was out of control. My short answer in our conversation was that I believed that one of our jobs as educators was to be able to engage an outsider's interpretation. We need to be able to talk about how the chaos of a good learning environment works for our diverse learners. My approach to doing that includes giving accounts of student learning through descriptions and reflections on what was observed and what was experienced. In the following paragraphs we take a closer look into Ms. Rosario's classroom and reflect on some of the things that we find there.

Ms. Rosario's Technology Integrated Classroom

I arrived early to Ms. Rosario's class one morning and was able to observe her working with her students at the front of her room on the carpet. The interactive white board was on and she had a Windows Media player application window open on the laptop that was connected to the interactive white board. Ms. Rosario was wearing a microphone around her neck that projected her voice through the classroom audio system speakers mounted at the front of the classroom. The sound of her voice was all encompassing it reminded me of the sales people at the convention trade shows who used similar devices to convince crowds to stop and consider what they were selling. The students were used to her using the device and were focused on her, I marvelled at how calm and relaxed her voice was. She didn't have to strain to maintain an increased volume that would eventually cause her voice to become shrill. I wondered if she was aware of how inviting her voice was.

Ms. Rosario explained to the students that she was going to play an audio recording of the author of Paper Bag Princess reading the story aloud. They would be doing a project where they would make paper puppets on Popsicle sticks and use them to practice retelling the story to someone at home. She asked the students some quick questions smoothly using well-known cooperative learning techniques to refresh their memories of the story and directed them to pay attention to differences they might hear in the version of the story that the author was reading. She clicked on the Play button and Windows Media player started displaying its Visualizer. The Visualizer application generated lines and colors emerged and transformed on the screen in time with the author's voice. The students turned toward the interactive white board transfixed by the colorful abstract images. The author's voice boomed from the speakers as he animated his story with a loud grumpy dragon voice, a high-pitched, determined princess voice and a hapless and dopey prince voice. I wondered if the students would be distracted by all of the special effects, but we were rewarded with a thorough question and answer session afterwards when the students demonstrated that they had been paying attention to the story.

Ms Rosario repeated her instructions to the students, they were to use construction paper and Popsicle sticks to create the puppets of the characters in the story and then use them to retell the story. She dismissed the students from the carpet and they returned to their tables. Students who performed the duties of "Table monitors" went to shelves near the windows to retrieve paper and plastic bins full of scissors, glue, rulers and markers. The room became noisy as the students organized themselves to work on the project. Ms. Rosario opened another window on the interactive white board and displayed a digital timer, the students had 15 minutes to create their puppets.

I wandered around the room taking pictures of the things on the walls and the technologies that were available to the students. The room contained a history of technology in education. Old technology in the form of headsets and tape players sat on a shelf a few feet away from six relatively new Dell *computers that were connected to the Internet and organized in groups of three on two tables with an ink-jet printer between them. On more than one occasion I had observed students working independently on the computers, either word processing or using a free Internet-based typing practice program. I had even observed students helping each other to problem solve the tasks of saving and retrieving files. The students had e-mail accounts and Ms. Rosario had trained them to go to a Blog that she maintained to give them another resource to find homework assignments.*

My eyes wandered around the room. Kagan posters (from the Kagan cooperative learning system), a word wall, student work, writing rubrics, writing process posters, books organized in color coded bins indicating level and genre, student notebooks and folders organized in more bins. There was also a cluttered but organized teacher's desk with a plan book open to the current day. A great deal of work went into putting posters on the walls and keeping everything in the bins orderly. There was a student job chart and a student behavior chart. Ms. Rosario made students responsible for maintaining various aspects of classroom life and she used the behavior chart as part of her reward system. On a bookshelf along a wall of curtain covered windows there was a bin with u-shaped white PVC pipes. Out of curiosity, I asked Ms. Rosario about the pipes and she explained that she had attended a workshop that suggested using a similar plastic pipe to have students listen to themselves as they read aloud while holding the pipe to ear and mouth the way they would a phone. I tried it and my voice sounded magnified and like it was coming out of a seashell. Ms. Rosario explained that the colorful plastic pipe that was used at the workshop was $11.00 and that the PVC pipe from her local home improvement store was $1.00. There was a lot of evidence in the room that Ms. Rosario was smart, hard working and willing to put the things she learned in professional development workshops to good use. I saw that she was able to integrate technology into the classroom in efficient and helpful ways and she was creative. I also knew that she participated in school wide events, cooperated with teachers on her grade and contributed to the various committees that were active in the school. I was impressed and proud of Ms. Rosario's work, she wanted my help, she was interested in doing more than she was currently doing, I was looking forward to continuing to develop our work together.

Seeing Students Differently Through Video

While looking through some digital video that I had download to my computer from an inexpensive digital camera one pair of students in Ms. Rosario's class caught my attention. Two girls were rehearsing lines from a script, each had a word processed copy of a script that one of them had written and they were practicing their lines facing each other while sitting on stools at the front of the classroom. Around us other students were rehearsing scenes and revising scripts. The two students were intent on rehearsing their lines, one student, I'll call her

Jane, was fairly aggressive in her approach to getting the other to say a certain line correctly. The other student, Sally, kept missing the line she was supposed to say and at one point Jane took the script away from Sally and pointed to where Sally needed to look to read the line. At the same time Jane was also aware of my presence and looked directly at the camera and smiled slyly as she waited for Sally to finish the next line of the script. Several things jumped out at me while I watched the video of the scene, Jane and Sally seemed very committed to practicing the scene with each other, they seemed to be able to ignore most of the distractions around them, and they were very aware of the audience (me with a video camera). I showed the video to Ms. Rosario and while she was not surprised at Jane's aggressiveness she was surprised that Jane could maintain her focus for so long (a three-minute scene). At the time that the scene actually happened, I had not thought much about what Jane and Sally were doing other than to be vaguely aware that they, like many other students seemed to be heavily invested in the performance activity.

Seeing Through the Lens of a Test

Ms. Rosario is in her late 20's she is Latina and works with predominately Black and Latino children in a Jersey City public school in New Jersey. She and I have known each other for many years and she asked me to do a technology project with her students. She got clearance from her principal and we got to work on determining what the project would be. We settled on a project that involved using the digital video camera to produce a DVD of student performances. The students would use the computers to revise scripts and print copies so they wouldn't have to share scripts during rehearsals. We would video student performances of the scripts and put together something that could be shown around the school and to parents.

When we started the project it was early in the school year and the students were focused on writing memoirs and producing detailed descriptions. Ms. Rosario carved out about 2 hours each week for me to come in and work with two groups of students. We encouraged the students to use the material from the memoirs and their lives to create scenes. We emphasized that the characters they were writing needed to tell the audience what was going on by providing as much detail as possible.

During our many conversations about her class Ms. Rosario conveyed the following: "My homeroom students are sweet and they follow instructions well but they struggle on the standardized tests. My other group does well on the standardized test but they don't work well as a group they seem to get more work done working individually." Ms. Rosario's 3rd grade is departmentalized, she teaches literacy for her 3rd grade class and for another 3rd grade class. Another teacher provides math instruction for both classes. The students switch classrooms when they start the instructional time for math or literacy. Over the weeks that I worked with Ms. Rosario's students I thought about her contradiction, students that were a good group struggled with the standardized test. Students that did well on the test struggled as a group. I thought about how teachers are pushed by their circumstances to using test results as the predominant means to evaluate, determine and justify what needed to be done for students.

As the school year progressed Ms. Rosario and her peers began to exhibit signs of stress about upcoming tests. She was planning on preparing for the test using all means available including going "old school," this included memorization drills and practice tests. During this time the way she and her peers talked about their classrooms and their students changed. The teachers became very intense, identifying every learning problem that each student had and they fretted about how nothing seemed to be working. They identified problems with the curriculum and problems with the conditions that they were working in. They worried about how their performance would be judged based on student performance and they worried about the consequences. They complained that the students they had were below grade level when they got them and that they would still be below grade level when they took a test that they couldn't possibly pass. They complained that their students did better with support but that the support was taken away when they sat for a test. As I listened to the litany and nodded my head in agreement I also became frustrated. Ms. Rosario couldn't hear what I was saying to her. I was telling her that there was nothing that she could do to fix any of the things that she was complaining about and that she shouldn't be stressing herself out. She looked at me plainly frustrated and with all the intensity that she had, asked "Then what do I do?"

It's hard to respond to someone who is immersed in problems in a way that is satisfying or immediately perceived as helpful. "Don't worry about it," is not an answer that anyone thinks is helpful. Similarly, pointing out that all of the educators that are currently working on these exact problems do not seem to be able to solve the problems either, does nothing to alleviate feeling frustrated and worried about what is happening with your classroom and your career. I understand the concerns. I suggested that Ms. Rosario try not to make herself or her students miserable during their preparation for the test and that perhaps she could work on emotions and getting students to articulate (maybe perform would have been a better thing for me to say) how they were feeling and what they were struggling with.

Ms. Rosario didn't think that emotions were a problem. She also didn't think that the students knew why they were struggling. When I asked Ms. Rosario why emotions didn't matter she said that, "you just have to work harder to pass the tests." When I pressed her about how she felt when answering questions that she didn't know the answer to she admitted to feeling anxious and using that feeling to work harder. When I asked her about how her students felt about taking the tests, she said that she did all kinds of things to make them feel comfortable and relaxed. I felt Ms. Rosario's frustration and I felt my own, she was pushing back and I felt that I had not done enough to prepare us for this conversation.

Ms. Rosario and I were disagreeing in an interesting way. We were trying to do two different things in our work together. She decided that working harder was the solution to stress and anxiety about knowing things and demonstrating achievement. I struggled to find a performatory direction to give her, given what she was immersed in. Apparently, from Ms. Rosario's perspective, nothing I was advocating was of any immediate use in solving the problems she was describing. Ms. Rosario wanted answers to the problem of getting her students to pass a high stakes standardized exam. I believed that the problem of students passing a standardized exam had little to do with her ability to teach or her students' capacity to learn. I could see that Ms. Rosario's enthusiasm for showing up to work had disappeared and that how she was relating to her students now included a great deal of anxiety, frustration, fear and anger. I wanted to help Ms. Rosario reorganize her relationship to what was happening to her and her students but that was not going to happen in one conversation. I was also fairly certain that nothing that she could do in the weeks leading up to the test would yield miraculous gains in student achievement. If such a thing were possible using any means available, the problem would be solved already! In the next section we will step away from Ms. Rosario's class to look at problems more broadly.

RESISTANCE IS...A PROBLEM

The resistance that is most prevalent in my work with students and other teachers is the resistance they have to giving up on seeing everything as a problem to solve. The litany of complaints that Ms. Rosario and thousands of good teachers like her articulate are the daily realities they experience that reveal that despite all of the solutions, i.e. more qualified teachers, longer school days, higher standards, more testing, more money, longer school years, etc., they are still engaged in problems that they have no solutions for. Those problems are described as children lacking adequate health care, poverty, deteriorating communities, race and class inequities, lack of transparency in the political process, declining property values, violence in the home and community, and it goes on an on. Schools are not designed to address the ills of the communities that they exist in nor are they necessarily prepared to utilize outside resources that may be available. It seems fairly obvious to me that the way forward should include re-thinking the need to deal with "problems" at school.

Vanishing of Problems – A Philosophical Digression

Ludwig Wittgenstein was a 20th century Austrian philosopher who is well known for two philosophical works, the first is Tractatus Logico-Philosophicus and the other is Philosophical Investigations. In his earlier work, Tractatus, his goal was to work out a philosophical approach that corrects misconceptions about language through abstract logic. In his later book, Philosophical Investigations, published after his death in 1951 he rejects much of what was in Tractatus and introduces language-games, a way of playing with language, to help clear up the "muddles" that are created when we are stuck or encounter contradictions that can be traced to the meanings of words and the ways we are using language. Most of my understanding about the work of Wittgenstein comes from performing philosophizing (doing philosophy by playing language-games) in performatory social therapeutic learning environments and reading books by Newman and Holzman (Holzman & Mendez, 2003; Newman & Holzman, 1997).

My favorite quote of Wittgenstein's is from Tractatus

We feel that even if all possible scientific question be answered, the problems of life have still not been touched at all. Of course, there is then no question left, and just this is the answer. The solution of the problem of life is seen in the vanishing of this problem.

Playing with Ms. Rosario's Litany

Here's how I use Wittgenstein's ideas and performance to create a "vanishing" of Ms. Rosario's problems in school. It's easiest to think about what is going on as a session of "let's pretend" this is what we said.

The Setting:

Jim and Ms. Rosario are sitting at his dinning room table talking about her students. She is anxious because she needs to start preparing them for testing and she has told Jim that she doesn't have time for the "enrichment program" they were running during her literacy block once every other week or so.

Ms. Rosario: I'm going to go "old school" with these kids.

Jim: What does "old school" mean?

Ms. Rosario: Memorization, drills, test prep.

Jim: Does going "old school" mean that what you do the rest of the time is a waste?

Ms. Rosario: No it's not a waste, I'm teaching the curriculum, using all of the resources I'm told to use, but I have to get these kids to pass the test.

Jim: Why bother doing anything else if the goal is to "pass the test" and going "old school" is the way to do it?

Ms. Rosario: Look, I just have to get them through this. I'm going to try everything, but sometimes memorizing is all you need to do to get an answer right.

Jim: Memorization and drills are "old school" but how many questions is that going to work for?

Ms. Rosario: Well then, what do YOU suggest I do?"

Jim: Think about what you are doing differently.

Ms. Rosario: What do you mean think about what I am doing differently? What other way is there to think about it? There's a test coming, you work hard, you get ready for it and you take it.

Jim: You don't have a choice here.

Ms. Rosario:	What do you mean?
Jim:	You are expected to do Test Prep for several weeks before the test and part of that will include going "old school" correct?
Ms. Rosario:	Correct.
Jim:	And you do what is expected of you correct?
Ms. Rosario:	Well of course, my job is on the line here, I have to show that I am doing my best to get those kids to pass.
Jim:	Do you think if you do everything correctly as you are told, that they will all pass?
Ms. Rosario:	No, Some of them are just too far behind, there's not enough time to get them caught up and some of them... I don't know what's wrong with them. I got three kids that showed up within the last month. They don't do homework, they can't stay in their seats, it's like I've got to start from scratch with them and... (Jim interrupts)
Jim:	So what is upsetting you is that some of them will fail no matter what you do and you have no choice in the matter.
Ms. Rosario:	I don't understand what you are talking about. I have a lot of choices I have to make.
Jim:	Yes, and refusing to participate in testing students that you know will fail isn't one of them. In other words, you cannot opt out, you can't say no, you have no choice here.
Ms. Rosario:	Well, they have to be tested and I have to be the one who tests them.
Jim:	Yes.
Ms. Rosario:	This is not getting me anywhere! You are not helping me.
Jim:	Right, this won't get us anywhere.
Ms. Rosario:	Why aren't you helping me? You said you would help me.
Jim:	I am trying to help you see that there is no solution to the problem that you are describing.
Ms. Rosario:	How am I describing the problem?
Jim:	You describe the problem in terms that limit the possibilities.
Ms. Rosario:	The possibilities of what?
Jim:	The possibility that you and your students are doing anything other than the test.
Ms. Rosario:	That's ridiculous! Teaching is about more than preparing for the test.
Jim:	I agree.

Ms. Rosario: (frustrated) I'm just so angry. I try so hard and they try so hard, and I don't want them to fail and I don't want to fail and … (Jim interrupts)

Jim: I understand.

Ms. Rosario: I don't know what I am going to do...

Jim: That's a good place to start.

Ms. Rosario: What? I don't know...(interrupting again)

Jim: Exactly!

Ms. Rosario: What! Now you're making fun of me?

Jim: Never. The problem just vanished.

Ms. Rosario: What do you mean, the problem, you mean the test"

Jim: No, you thinking that going "old school" is the solution to a problem that you know and can't seem to solve.

Ms. Rosario: Oh! You're making me crazy!

Jim: Yes, these types of problems make us crazy. It sounds to me that with going "old school" you are trying to reach for something that you believe worked in the past and might be useful now. You also know that there is too much your students need to overcome and that the situation is too complex. There is nothing that can help in time for the test. Everything that you know will not help you to a solution and that is a pretty painful place for a human being to be.

Ms. Rosario: (shaking her head in surrender and gesturing with her hand) Okay. What now?

Jim: We can start by creating learning environments. I've found it very helpful in working my way out of the contradictions at school. I think you and your students will feel better about what you are doing, including taking the test, and in the long term, I'm confident that all of you will learn and develop. You'll set yourself up to think creatively and critically about what you are doing with students.

Ms. Rosario: What do you mean by "create a learning environment"? I don't KNOW what you mean by that.

Jim: Well...we'll create what we mean by that.

Curtain.

The Playful Dialogue

My postmodern play ended without a resolution. In the play we get to play around with the meanings of words and phrases like "old school." We can take our time and look at the situation from a different set of lenses or perspectives. It's difficult to do that in a live conversation, it takes some training to be patient enough and playful enough to work through deeply held understandings and meanings and casually deconstruct them. This is a barrier that I have experienced in conversations with people who may have a different set of understandings. I can't assume that I can challenge a deeply held understanding of the world without provoking emotional responses on all sides. A made up play (we are pretending) about real life, helps to create an environment where the playful dialogue can be had and reflected upon.

Wittgenstein's method, the language-game, helps with seeing things differently. The vanishing of the problem helps us move on. In the play a change of subject from passing "the test" to "I don't know what to do?" is seized upon to build the conversation in a different direction. My colleagues at the Institute and I have had more success in working with teachers on learning to "think outside of the box" when we have engaged them "outside of the school." In real life Ms. Rosario became immersed in test prep and testing and had no time to continue our project in the classroom. We did figure out what we could do together and that included her participation in an educational seminar I was a part of outside of school and her ongoing interest in the book I was writing.

HIGHLIGHTS

- Technology integration in Ms. Rosario's classroom is depicted in the context of literacy projects.
- What counts as technology integration in the classroom is called in to question as various items, such as tape recording machines, PVC pipes, bulletin boards and scissors are still useful in a 21st century classroom along with computers, electronic white boards and wireless sound systems.
- A play is presented in a playful manner to help achieve a different way of looking at problems.
- A philosophical digression introduces Wittgenstein, philosophizing and language-games as a type of performance to help with working through conflicting meanings and contradictions.
- The history of the performatory intervention provides a familiar accounting of how demands coming from outside of the classroom impact on the decisions of teachers and the emotional environment that is produced.
- Technology use provides multiple opportunities facilitate collaboration and to provide teachers with opportunities to see students perform differently.
- Different points of view are revealed when video recording is interpreted.

QUESTIONS FOR DISCUSSION

1. Can you identify a problem that doesn't seem to have solutions? If so what are the characteristics of the problem?
2. Human beings design technology to solve problems. Think about a technology that has become obsolete. Was that technology replaced by something else or

did the problem it solved vanish? Is the technology still useful? Is there a cost-benefit analysis that explains why an older technology shouldn't be used even though it still technically functions?

3. Can you think of a problem that "vanished" when the circumstances changed? What changed or what events triggered the change? What did people do when they perceived the change in circumstances?

4. Would writing a short play or scene about a conversation you had change what you thought about the real conversation?

5. What challenges are posed by the use of qualitative data such as video?

ORGANIZING THE LEARNING ENVIRONMENT

I started my career in education naively believing that the positive experiences that I'd had with inner city youth in after-school programs would be available in a public school setting. That turned out not to be the case, and I turned to Lois Holzman and the faculty at the East Side Institute (the Institute), where she was the director, for support and for training in coping with the frustration, anger, isolation and assorted trials and tribulations of new urban public school teachers.

One of the things that I learned at the Institute was that I had to take responsibility for my teaching practice. These chapters describe that practice and part of taking responsibility for my teaching practice has been to make it public by writing about it and by organizing others to observe, comment, and participate in it. The limitations, power differentials, and generally oppressive, non-developmental features of schooling are part of our daily experience in school and are often taken for granted. Some people refer to the difficulties of school as "a rite of passage." Performance, improvisation and technology allow me to do something creative with my students and allow us to transform our experience of the schooling environment. Our transformed experiences make many of the things that we take for granted visible.

The process that is undertaken by my students to produce multimedia artifacts includes, collaborative group work, interpretation of the project requirements, struggling and playing with the technology, struggling to organize the activity, providing leadership to emerging situations, and going back and forth about what needs to be or can be created. These features of the learning environment are not easily visible in one classroom visit or in a PowerPoint presentation or even by asking about it. In this chapter I provide a description of the process and the struggles that we faced in the technology classroom as we produced multimedia artifacts. I have elected to talk about the work that I have done with a 12:1 special education class because the need to build or develop the social and emotional aspects of the learning environment are most evident here, and are key to being able to use technology creatively in the classroom.

A Technology Teacher in the 12:1 Classroom

I worked at Manhattan Middle School for four years, during that time one of my assignments included teaching the 12:1 special education class (12 students, a mix of 6th and 7th grade, 1 teacher). Linda, Gregory, Tina and Philip were special education students in the 12:1 class. They each had an Individualized Education Program (IEP) that detailed learning challenges and contained required modifications to learning tasks and assessments. The IEP is a legal document; in practice the IEP guarantees that the student is related to as an individual with specific needs that must be met by the school. The various diagnosis and treatments in the IEP function to bring clarity and reinforcement to understandings of the nature of the disability in the context of schooling. Only special education teachers and administrators are privy the information in the IEP.

While I was learning to work with these students as a group, the individuals in the group each accepted or rejected my various offers to become engaged in various activities. It was hard to find things that everyone in the group was willing to agree with. The work with this class was emotionally draining and there was a disproportionate amount of chaos to engage given the relatively few students in the class. I loved it when we were able to accomplish things together and I eventually became very happy with what we were doing. I discovered that creating a more intimate environment to support learning was possible (not always and not easily) in the 12:1 special education setting.

Offers

An offer is something that a performer does, some form of speech or a gesture with which another performer or the ensemble creates a scene (Lobman & Lundquist, 2007). An offer may be scripted, what you would expect, and/or it might be improvisational or unexpected. Human beings make scripted and improvisational offers all the time. Sometimes unexpected offers are accepted and a scene is creatively transformed and the performers become engaged in continuing to create some enjoyable, or productive activity together. Sometimes offers are blocked or rejected and the performers (teacher and students) have difficultly continuing to work together and the environment can become stressful, angry and even violent. Many scripted offers are useful for getting us through the day and creating a sense of familiarity and order. Sometimes the offers are so scripted that the performers can anticipate the exchange and the conclusion and simply go through the motions as if trapped in an endlessly repeating loop.

I work to accept all offers, good, bad and scripted, from my students to create what we are doing together in a way that involves everyone. On occasions where I've had to resort to excluding a child from the group, I consider it to be a failure of the group, with my leadership, to create the ensemble performance or methodological tools that the situation required. Sometimes we failed to create the performance because we hadn't developed sufficiently as a group to create what we needed. In other words, there were things that were outside of the group's zone of proximal development (ZPD). In those instances what we needed was more experience and more diversity in our group to help us to go further together.

One idea that was difficult to challenge in our group was the idea of disability. My students really owned their disabilities and would resist my attempts to push them beyond whatever they understood to be the limit of what they believed they could do. Their actions indicated that they wanted to be dependent on me and they demanded that I attend to their needs. They wanted me to see their disabilities the way that they had learned to see them in school. They wanted me to stick with the program, as they understood it that was their offer.

Just to clarify, I never asked students to do things that they could not do on their own. I pushed them to *participate, to offer more towards creating the activities that they could do with the assistance of others.* The following citation from Holzman's earlier work (published as Hood) in *Psychological Investigations* helped me understand how I was seeing or not seeing disabilities in the classroom environments that I created with my students.

> ...we saw a complex, socially constructed cultural scene involving many people and institutions. We concluded that learning disability for example, did not exist outside of or separate from the interactive work (joint activity) that people do that, intentionally or not, creates "displays" of disability (Hood, McDermott, & Cole, 1980; McDermott & Hood, 1982). (Holzman & Mendez, 2003, p. 40)

If learning disability does not exist outside of or separate from interactive work, this means that it's always there, part of what we are doing, and sometimes we create the conditions for disability to be visible. Disability becomes visible in school when we design an educational task that is beyond the ability of a relatively small number of students. For example, if we design a task that only left-handed students could complete we would determine that the task was poorly designed because the majority of students could not complete the task. However, if we design tasks that all right handed students could complete, we might treat the left handed students as special cases and modify the task for them. The "disability" of left-handedness would be a "culturally constructed object" (Mehan, 1988) that was put on display in school.

When we choose to design activities for groups to accomplish, the issue of individual handedness or disability disappears (although left-handedness is still there) because someone in the group will probably have the required handedness to complete the task that requires a particular handedness and the larger group context provides opportunities for all (hopefully) to contribute to the activity in different ways. This issue of "disability" is not limited to the visibility of disability, or the quality of instructional design. How the child with a "disability" is represented via the various discourses of a school is an issue as well. The political discourse, how we talk about the children, shapes and connects what happens in the everyday setting to the broader discourse about disability (Mehan, 1993). This makes it extremely difficult to talk about children designated as disabled in any way other than the way that is connected to the "official discourse" that labels them as disabled. In the sections that follow, I present some of the children I worked with and I use some of the official discourse to describe them. I also describe them as performers of technical activities such as e-mail and movie making and as members and leaders of a group.

E-mail as a Back Channel

Linda is Latina, is easy to work with, follows directions, and tries to pursue her tasks to completion. She is easily distracted by other students, and will follow the crowd if she sees that everyone else is engaged in off task behavior. She is absent frequently, is often sullen, and is capable of becoming violent with her peers when angered. When I started working with Linda and the rest of her class I taught them to use e-mail and made checking e-mail part of our routine. I sent each student the following personalized e-mail.

> *Hi Linda,*
>
> > *I hope you are having a good time being at school. We are glad to have you. You can always use e-mail to communicate with your teachers. If you have any problems let us know! You are doing great work in class. I look forward to working with you.*
>
> *- Jim*

A week or so later, Linda walked into the room, clearly upset. I asked her if she wanted to talk and she said no. I said, it was okay and asked her to check her e-mail and continue with her normal routine. Linda sent me an e-mail message.

> *Daer jim,*
>
> > *I no you want to no what happen will me and Philip was in the science room doing hour work I was trying to help him but he got very mad for no reasion and said in a laod voice can you let me speak and I said sorry and he got mad agen and that why I was not happy*
>
> *From Linda*

Then I received the following:

> *hi Jim*
>
> > *I am not feeling good to day and I think I am not going to feel good to the end of the school year...*
>
> *Linda,*

I replied later:

> *Linda,*
>
> > *I'm sorry you are not feeling well. To the end of the year sounds like a really long time to not feel well. Is there any way I can help you?*
>
> *- Jim*

Linda received my response in class and indicated that she was feeling better about her situation. I learned from the special education teachers during these e-mail interactions that Linda and Philip had a history together that started when they were in a special education class in elementary school. I noticed in class that Linda went out of her way to offer assistance to peers and that she was very attentive to what is going on in the room. After the incident described above I observed that Linda continued to interact with Philip and offered to help him on occasion. Linda demonstrated that e-mail could be a back channel for communicating with teachers in a personal way when a face-to-face conversation was beyond her ability at that particular moment. Linda was also an early adopter of the social networking software I introduced to the rest of the sixth grade and she used the software to connect with students outside of the special education class.

The Behavior Problem

It is very easy for teachers to label Philip, who is Latino, as the troublemaker or as the bad kid in the class. He can disrupt the classroom by arguing with the teacher, making fun of students, and inciting other students to similar behavior before he has even taken a seat in the classroom. In addition, to his "behaviors" he is morbidly obese, has difficulty walking because of his obesity, doesn't read very well, and refuses to do things for himself. I noticed Philip on the very first day of school. My first impression: "This poor little guy is huffing and puffing on the first landing on his way up four flights of stairs, how is he going to do this everyday for the next 3 years?"

It became very clear, early in the school year that Philip was willing to go head to head with me on who was running the classroom. After a few negative encounters I decided to back off and reorganize my style of running the classroom so that Philip and other students could take turns being explicitly in charge. In the general education classroom we create an environment where I can have my back turned away from the larger group to work with individuals or smaller groups. This form of distributed leadership in the general education setting did not require my constant attention. Students were socially developed enough to provide sufficient levels of leadership and cooperation to their independent activities. I could not initially do this in the 12:1 class. What we initially were able to create in the 12:1 class was a form of distributed leadership that allowed me to be in charge of whoever was "in charge."

I reasoned that Philip and I would have fewer opportunities to argue if I was in charge of him and others being in charge. It had been my experience that students who were accustomed to getting poor grades and calls home were more likely to challenge my authority and engage me in an escalating conflict in the classroom. I had many occasions to watch Philip routinely tell adults what they wanted to hear and then proceed to do whatever he wanted. I'd been a party to these interactions with other students and I was determined to work for an alternative.

Being "in charge" for Philip and the other students included running the class meeting and being or choosing the leader for games or other group activities. A leader would ask each member of the group what they planned to accomplish during independent project time. The leader also selected the order in which students would be dismissed from the meeting to retrieve laptops. In addition, the leader could plan a future opportunity to lead by meeting with me to learn how to play a new game or plan a favorite activity.

What I offered Philip and the other students was the opportunity to create new choices that included using computers, providing positive leadership in the classroom, and building LEGO robotics models. I learned that Philip was interested in LEGOs when he responded to an e-mail asking him to tell me about an activity he enjoyed. When his mother came in for Parent-Teacher night we had a conversation about his interests.

Mother: *Sometimes he will be very aggressive, he thinks people will give him trouble before they actually do anything.*

Jim: *I noticed that about him.*

Mother: *He wants to be in control of everything.*

Jim: *I noticed that about him also, I decided to put him in charge of running the class meeting, he liked that. I need him to understand that he can't be mean to the other kids and still be in charge of the meeting.*

Mother: *How is he mean?*

Jim: *He teases Gregory, he makes fun of the way he talks and he yells at Linda.*

Mother: *Oh, he calls Linda his girlfriend.*

Jim: *Linda doesn't like to be yelled at by him, she even wrote me an e-mail about it. Please talk to him.*

Mother: *I will talk to him.*

Jim: *I noticed that Philip is really good at working with LEGOs*

Mother: *Oh yes, he's always been very good at that.*

Jim: *He can make some pretty complicated projects, not everybody can do that, even with a diagram. We have the beginnings of an engineer.*

Mother: *Oh yes, and he likes to draw. Has he shown you his drawings?*

Jim: *No I didn't know that. I'll ask him to show me. I want to use his interest in LEGOs and drawing to get him to work on more projects. Maybe even some LEGO robotics. Has he ever done that before?*

Mother: *No, but that would be very good if you could get him to do that.*

Jim: *Okay then, that's what we'll try.*

Claymation[1] Movies

Gregory was an average sized 11-year old with braces, fair skin, dark eyes and dark hair. He was what you would consider cute, and exhibited the behaviors associated with much younger children. For example, on a class trip he was observed holding hands with his father and skipping. He was very intelligent, often spoke in funny voices, and would utter sentences in a rapid-fire fashion. I was told that he had a form of Asperger's Syndrome and had a history of being teased by other children. Gregory was the first student to respond to me in a positive and decisive way on the first day of class. My question was, "What would you like to do in this class?" The other students took a week or more to respond. Gregory wrote me an e-mail that said, "I want to do Claymation." I had no prior experience with Claymation so I helped Gregory do an Internet search on the subject and I asked him to find information on how to proceed. He had some prior experience with Claymation in a camp that he attended. We worked together to produce his Claymation movie. When I met with his parents we discussed his progress in class.

Father: *I don't know what you did, but you taught Gregory how to embarrass his mother.*

Jim: *What do you mean?*

Father: *He's gotten so good at the computer that he can do things his mother doesn't know how to do.*

Jim: *Oh, I see.*

Mother: *How is Gregory in your class?*

Jim: *He is absolutely wonderful. Did he show you his movie? He finished it yesterday?*

Mother: *No he didn't.*

Jim: *Ask him to show you, he has it on his flash drive. He made a Claymation movie. He decided he wanted to do that, and we figured out how by doing some research on the Internet, then I got him some clay and he made the backgrounds, then I showed him how to work the camera. He did a lot of work.*

Father: *What's Claymation?*

Gregory was very dependent on my feedback during the initial stages of the Claymation project. He asked many questions about the materials he would need and about what his project could be about. "Can I make the Claymation about a fish that turns into a man? Can there be an evil wizard that he has to fight?" I noticed that Gregory was very detail oriented. Once Gregory became comfortable with the tools of his project, clay, digital camera, computer, and the movie making application, he was able to focus on his project during 40 minutes of class time over the course of several weeks. During this period he would sit by himself, largely ignoring everything else that went on in the room. He was meticulous in his creation of the clay characters and the sets. He took over a hundred still pictures and then loaded them into movie making software and adjusted the time slices for each picture. When he completed his project he was proud of his work and was willing to display it to his classmates.

During the project Gregory would occasionally talk out loud in his normal speaking voice about what he was doing while he was doing it. "Now I need to put this right here and next I have to find the pin and... hey Jim, I can't find the pin! ...Oh...never mind, there it is. Now I have put the lantern on the paper with the pin..." I was listening to Gregory's speech while I was across the room working with another student. The room had been quiet, everyone was engaged in some activity and I noticed that Gregory was talking but not to anyone in particular. When he called my name I became more attentive and I then realized that he went back to talking to no one in particular when he found the pin and resumed his activity. This may be an example of Gregory's private speech; Vygotsky (1978) recognizes that there is a relationship between speech and action in young children and this may be an indicator that Gregory was experiencing a challenging task. Several weeks after Gregory completed the project I asked him what had been hard for him during his Claymation project. He said that setting up the backgrounds (the miniature sets for the clay characters) had been the hardest (this was when the pin incident had occurred).

I have not been privy to the contents of Gregory's IEP and it is not my intention to diagnose Gregory or draw conclusions about whether his private speech disappears as he gains mastery and whether occurrences could be used to gauge developmental milestones. The literature is clear that private speech is "helpful" (Winsler, Abar, Feder, Schunn, & Rubio, 2007) to his development, and it is helpful to understand the private speech may indicate that the physical aspect of the project was what Gregory found challenging. It was interesting, even though it wasn't a central focus of my interest.

The three students described above accomplished some new things on their own while I had other students who were also in need of my attention and who were struggling to complete tasks. Some of my other students were not part of a group and I could not support all of us to go much further within the 12:1 framework as 12 individuals. In the next section Tina, a student who struggles to complete academic tasks emerges as a leader and helps to build the group.

BUILDING THE GROUP

I met with the 12:1 special education students twice a week for one hour for the entire year. The students travelled outside of their regular classroom to see me and I realized early on that I would need some time at the beginning of class to transition them into the room. We settled on a group meeting and a group activity that would take up the first 10-20 minutes of the period. The remaining 30 or 40 minutes of class time would be used for project work using technology in groups and individually. During that time I would move around the room working with groups and individuals on their projects.

Through the school year, as the group developed, my students challenged me in direct and personal ways. This was possible because I opened up the environment for change. I was willing to change my teaching practices and provide students with opportunities to respectfully (and sometimes disrespectfully) challenge the way things were. As I learned new things about them, they effectively modified my teaching practice through their insistence on conducting the classroom activities their way. This included occasional refusals to work, and their willingness to hold me to administering to the group according to their standards of fairness. My agenda, to the extent that it was obvious to them, was routinely pushed to the side if it did not align with theirs. In handing out opportunities for students to provide leadership, I had let the genie out of the bottle and they had no interest in allowing me to monopolize being "in charge" of who was "in charge."

A female African American student named Tina brought this home for me. She had become one of my favorite leaders and I had created opportunities for her to be class leader at the expense of others getting a regular chance to take a turn leading. Tina was an enormous help to me with "class management issues," the girls automatically took their cues from her and Philip and the other boys respected her and rarely challenged her. She was also generous in her manner and she made it very easy for me to count on her. Tina admitted to me that she enjoyed being a leader but that certain situations made her uncomfortable and we agreed that any time such a situation presented itself that she could just let me take care of it. On several occasions she proved herself surprisingly adept at mediating conflicts between Philip and myself and helped me to see my own limitations and contradictions in certain situations.

> *One day during a class meeting, Philip raised the issue that I had not been fair in giving out leadership opportunities and I argued that I wasn't interested in being fair. I was feeling cranky that day and Philip started in on me almost immediately. I wanted the best leaders to lead so that I could move on to other goals. Other students who felt similarly cheated jumped into the conversation. When it was my turn to comment on this situation I asked for suggestions. I must have recognized that I had a revolution on my hands because I collected myself and started to perform being reasonable even though I still didn't feel that way. Tina suggested that we write down everyone's name on paper and randomly pick who would be the next leader. The students then pulled out paper, pencils, found a hat and had a drawing of names and the matter was resolved. Then I felt very reasonable and cooperative. I wish every revolution could go that smoothly.*

Most elementary school teachers recognize that picking names randomly is fair and an obvious classroom management tool that is used widely in elementary schools. It is clear that my students had those elementary school teachers and *recognized that they could create and use* a tool for producing a fair process when I asked for their suggestions (help). While a fair process didn't serve my short-term goals my students did understand that fairness was a priority in the environment. I had to admit that I had not been fair and that perhaps my goals, well intentioned as they were, did not justify being unfair, all leaders should learn this lesson.

During group work time my students would engage in a variety of tasks together and were able to complete them with varying degrees of success. Throughout the year we worked on playing games together. As a group, they were not very good at sustaining games like "Simon sez" or "Thumbs Up" or a variety of improvisation games that their drama teacher or I introduced them to. They were underdeveloped as listeners and performers of games that required following rules. They had difficulty agreeing on and conforming to the rules of the games that they played. Games that were led by the students and involved moving around the classroom were the most problematic. These games often degenerated into arguments, and physical altercations. Sometimes they looked so bad as a group I had to intervene by taking on the leadership role and continuing the game. Sometimes I let them come to their own conclusion by letting them take more time than planned to end an activity on their own terms. We often talked about why the game had ceased to be fun or had not gone well. They were good at understanding what had gone wrong, the challenge was having the collective discipline at the time something was happening to stop, regroup and try something different. Despite their lack of success at playing certain games together they were always willing to try again, and I was able to identify games and activities that they were good at.

I introduced an element of working against time to encourage learning how to get faster at games that required taking turns and paying attention. For example, collectively counting to 10 was a real challenge. In this game a random student would call out the first number and then a second student would call out the next number in order. If two students called out the same number simultaneously, the group had to start from the beginning. This game required listening and eye contact. Over the course of the year they did get better at this game and discovered techniques, such as waiting until everyone had a turn before calling out again. Working against their own best time provided motivation for getting better at playing and it also had the effect of creating pressure on everyone to do their part. One day while the students were playing a counting game, they discovered that if they said the numbers in a certain rhythm the counting was easier and faster. Gregory had the habit of talking in a funny voice that varied in pitch and timing. In this game, Gregory was exaggerating the timing of his cartoon character voice during his turn. His timing was throwing everyone off and the other students were getting upset. As a group, we asked him to use a voice that worked better, perhaps a normal sounding talking voice. This caused him to become upset and there were some tears. The group helped him to collect himself and he reluctantly complied. He seemed just as happy as everyone else when the group established a new record time when they resumed playing the game.

The students introduced a game that they had learned from the drama teacher that we called pass the beat, which involved rhythm and timing. Some students were very good at it and some not so good, but it seemed to be a game that produced a high level of entrainment even if a student was participating as an observer. Tina was poor at playing the game but she enjoyed listening to the rhythms of the game and she was brilliant at facilitating the game by subtly making moves while the game was being played to keep others from escalating disagreements. The other students would look to her to provide support with interpretation and enforcement of rules. In general the students were so focused when playing the game that they were not even distracted when Philip produced distractions that would normally result in everyone stopping the activity.

HOW WE FELT ABOUT IT

I enjoyed my work this group of students and I am proud of the work we did. We mostly had fun working on projects that the students picked out and helped determine deadlines for. Incomplete projects did happen and we talked about the factors that led to not finishing work. Many of my students were not comfortable with how it felt to work on a task that was hard for them. They felt frustrated and expected to fail. They could not see other routes to getting tasks done and they seemed to relate to frustration as if it were the antecedent to failure. I'd had numerous conversations with each of my students about getting work done and a common denominator was that they would prefer not to do a task than experience the humiliation of a failure to complete it. I'd learned not to place emphasis on project completion and focused on how the project was being worked on, which was another area in need of development. How they anticipated feeling about things seemed to be connected to what they would be willing to do.

Being Accepting

By giving Philip and Gregory the opportunity to express their interests I was able to get them engaged in an activity and add to my curriculum by responding to them in a serious and material way. Tina developed as a leader and was able to create opportunities for all, including myself, to have a different performance of authority and personal responsibility in the goings on in the learning environment. Linda used the technology to provide a new channel for social interaction that could transform her emotional disposition in the classroom. We all learned to be more accepting of each other and more supportive, the students demonstrated that they were capable of functioning as a cohesive group through their ongoing participation in games and collaborative projects.

There are those who have suggested that the relationships that I had established with these children could be used as leverage. For example, I could use my relationship with Philip to get Philip to work harder at reading or allow me to help him more. I think that such suggestions miss the focus of my interest in creating learning environments. My relationships with them were specific to the environment we had created in terms that we had all agreed to. Our relationships were not a transferable commodity that I could cash in to leverage another agenda.

What was Learned

All of my students in the special education class had demonstrated that they had developed their technical skills in significant ways with very little direct instruction. They learned to function in a collaborative environment that emphasized performing as a leader, being a good listener, being a helper, and being a responsible student. By comparing what they had been able to do at the beginning of the year, to what they could do at the end I could see their development. PowerPoint presentations that were incomplete after a whole class period in September were completed within minutes of a request in June. They had been exposed to and used Wikimedia software, course management software, e-mail, Internet browsers, Windows Moviemaker, Google maps, LEGO robotics, digital cameras, Dell Laptops and Mac Laptops and had worked hard on working as a group. This learning environment also was grounded in creating an atmosphere where student responsibility, i.e., selecting your own project, running the class meeting, determining the goal, demanding that the teacher be fair, etc., was methodologically supported by attending to the needs of the group (a new task, a different leader, a different conversation, and a new performance) instead of exclusively on the needs of the particular child. Individual needs were taken care of by the group with the support and guidance of different members of the group including the adult teacher. The group was engaged in interesting self-selected collective activity that included being aware that they needed to try to solve their own technical problems so that everyone could be supported.

While the movie making, LEGOs, e-mail and Internet technologies are not assistive technologies their use in student activities did transform the desire to work, play, perform, and get connected to adults and other students in the school community. These students provided some of the most rewarding experiences of my teaching career. Our use of technology provided opportunities to do the same old things in a new way and to create new things and new experiences. Our use of performance and improvisation provided us with the means of creating our own tools (collective conversations, agreements, creative projects) in the pursuit of new ways of doing things and creating, what I believed was, a more developmental learning environment.

Loss / Found on Facebook

I become emotional when I re-read this chapter aloud (curiously not as strongly when I read silently). In part it is because I am very proud of the work that we did together and because as important as the work is, it is not nearly enough and I find it frustrating that I could not do more to spread what we were doing into the other classroom settings. I also think that as I invested in building the group I developed a very complex emotional, relationship to my students. Our collective emotional investment in what we were doing together became very apparent when we lost a member of our group. Tina moved away very suddenly during the school year and we were all devastated by the loss. There were no goodbyes and no opportunities to process what her leaving meant. As a practical matter, what needed to be done was to rebuild the group. That process was intensely difficult, more difficult than I would have expected. We had group conversations about what Tina's loss had meant to the group. Other teachers and the guidance counselor had noticed a distinct difference in the character of this group of students without Tina. This was beyond my area of expertise but in this instance I would have said that our ZPD probably could have used some direction from a social therapist for help with our emotional pain. I was confronted with "behaviors" that were provocative, and more aggressive than I had previously seen from these students. Everyone agreed that

Philip was "much worse" and that Linda was "headed for trouble." Some of the other students seemed disoriented and much of my time was spent during the remainder of the school year learning to reorganize the group following this change. I'd lost students in other classrooms in mid-year before and it had never been so painful. I guess what we had built together, a learning environment where everyone could learn, was also a place where students and teachers developed strong emotional ties. Somehow, our emotional distance from each other, our indifference, and our lack of regard had been transformed; we had developed as caring human beings as was evident by our feelings of loss.

Two years after the events in this chapter Philip and several other students sought me out on Facebook and we have become friends. Philip got into a specialized art and design high school. When I visited the school earlier this year three of my younger former special education students saw me and warmly greeted me. They had transitioned in to general education inclusion classrooms and were looking forward to high school.

HIGHLIGHTS

– Games, theatrical improvisation and ideas on leadership and personal responsibility are featured as collective activities and goals in the creation of a learning environment.
– Detailed accounts of student activities and uses of technology are provided.
– Detailed descriptions provide context for the intense emotions that are produced as the group is created through ongoing interactions that help the development of the group.
– Technology provided the means to interact outside of normal classroom activity and provided opportunities for new possibilities (new kinds of student projects) in the classroom.
– The events and happenings in this chapter are viewed through a performatory lens and there is an ongoing and deliberate effort by the author to produce the learning environment using a performatory social therapeutic methodology.
– Diverse learners are provided with an opportunity to have input and control of what happens in the learning environment. They challenge authority and bring about change in classroom practices.

QUESTIONS FOR DISCUSSION

1. What are some of the challenges you face in creating learning environments for diverse students?
2. How do diverse learners challenge our assumptions about teaching and learning?
3. How does the language we use to talk about students impact on what we do with them?
4. Describe an instance that a student challenged your assumptions or your approach to a situation. Did the student change your practices? Why? Why not?

5. In the chapter the author claims that the students enacted a revolution. What do you think?
6. How do you think about frustration in a learning situation?

NOTES

[1] Claymation is animation that is created using figures made of clay and still photography. Slightly adjusting the pose of a clay figure and photographing the new position creates the illusion of movement when the images are placed in a digital video. Hundreds of pictures are needed for a one minute long movie.

TECHNOLOGY RICH LEARNING ENVIRONMENTS

In this chapter we meet young people who are engaged in learning that is connected to their interests. Their interests also coincide with membership in particular communities. First we meet Jessie who uses the Internet as a stage for her performance as a singer/guitarist. Then we meet Rubiks cube solving middle school students and uncover the secret of their success. Finally, we will meet Alex an expert at sports talk and a resource for his family and community. What these young people have in common is that they have deliberately made use of the Internet to acquire knowledge that was of interest to them. Access to technology rich environments that happen to incorporate some basic learning principles in their design provided different levels of membership in communities that would not have been otherwise possible for these young people.

Performing: Playing the Guitar

Jessie is fourteen years old and she is sitting in front of a digital video camera strumming her steel stringed acoustic guitar as she sings along with the popular song that is playing on the speakers of her iPod. Her bedroom is decorated with posters of young actors promoting their latest popular movies for teenaged girls. There are piles of clothes, dirty and clean, strewn around the room. Her bed is unmade, and a wireless phone handset, several stuffed dolls and some notebooks can be seen on top. She is looking into the mirror as she sings along to the song. On the desk next to the mirror is another pile of books, a hair curling iron and a hair straightening iron. This evening her shoulder length brown hair is straight with bangs across the front. She is sitting in front of a tall dresser and on the top, arranged neatly in two rows, is a collection of sunglasses next to a vase of artificial carnations, and two hairbrushes.

She has not kept track of how much time she has been practicing but for a period of about 6 months, she's been watching YouTube videos on the computer in the kitchen and on her iPod, of young people and original artists playing the songs that she is interested in. She has been able to download the lyrics and the tabs (chord notations) for the songs from the Internet and uses a guitar music reference book to get the chord fingering right. She has regularly stayed up late at night past bedtime quietly strumming and singing until she was happy with her musical performance. She also practiced rearranging her hair and clothing and adjusting the lighting in the room to prepare for recording her performance. She regularly borrows her father's digital video camera and asks not to be interrupted while she records.

After some trial and error she gets recordings that she likes. She uploads her recordings to her MySpace page and reports days later that she has hundreds of page views and many positive comments from friends about her videos. We know with certainty that she did not learn to use the technology in school and that she has no formal musical training on the guitar. Jessie's parents are enthusiastic about her interest in playing an instrument and offer to pay for lessons. She refused the offer and stated that she preferred to keep learning on her own. Jessie resists playing for her parents or friends. Her parents puzzle over that while they look at the video she produced for everyone on the Internet to watch.

Teaching Yourself and Learning on My Own

Is there really such a thing as "teaching yourself?" That's the question that I asked myself after several days of thinking and talking to others about Jessie's performance. Where was the more experienced peer or adult that was relating to the guitar player as "a head taller" than her actual level of development? What was the social context for the performance that she was engaged in? How was it possible for her to know and do more than when she had started if she was really just "teaching herself?" Why will she play for an Internet audience and not her parents? Can you actually be a performer if you are just pretending in front of your bedroom mirror?

ZPDs are created in a complex social environment and social environments can include people who are not in the room. A book, a bit of streaming video, a computer, an iPod, guitars, are all cultural artifacts that were made (produced, manufactured, created) by people not in the room. These cultural artifacts or tools were necessary for Jessie's guitar playing ZPD to be possible. The room itself, in the house, warmed by oil, paid for by the labor of adults and the complex social arrangements that make such things possible were all part of the creation of the guitar playing ZPD. Jessie is drawing on a rich socio-cultural history when she learning by herself.

Prior to her learning activity she had no repertoire of songs, or chords, she was limited to holding and strumming an open stringed guitar. Her interactions with Internet artists included being able to watch different artists engage in playing a song on the guitar or explaining some techniques. She also interacted with family members who could play the guitar by asking questions and watching them play. As she "taught herself" she produced a "creative imitation" (Vygotsky, 1978; Holzman, 2009) or pretended to be able to play and compared her performance to the performances she had seen and made decisions (conscious and unconscious) based on those comparisons. The various media sources, textual artifacts (lyrics, chord references), audio recordings, and video recordings provided the information that she needed to produce a performance of a particular song.

In order to retrieve and make sense of the resources that she is using on the Internet Jessie has to make use of search engines and must have a fair idea about the names (key words) of the things she is looking for so that she can download files and print what she will make use of. Songs that only have chord notations, for example G7 and no fingering charts will prompt her to continue her search for accompanying fingering charts. She will ask others for help, search the Internet and as a last resort ask her parents for a reference book. Once she knows where her fingers must be on all the chords she will practice producing a clear sound, making the chord transitions and duplicating the strum pattern. She will use music videos to learn the timing of the song. She will also identify "how to" videos that provide direct instruction and break down particularly complex songs that she wants to learn.

The instruments and recordings provide sensory experiences that are necessary for getting the sense that she is "doing it right." The online comments that she received from peers provide emotional support and performance feedback, "somebody likes it," "I'm doing it right." She presents that feedback to her parents and elicits more approval and produces good feelings about "learning it on my own." All of the songs that she learns produce ongoing changes in the ZPD. Her ongoing playing or pretending at being a video music star leads her to the moment when her father notices that the guitar needs to be tuned.

Prior to her father pointing out that the guitar is out of tune, Jessie had taken for granted the fact that someone else had tuned the guitar for her. She had not connected the difference in the sound she was making to the audio recordings she was using as being in the instrument and not in her playing. The activity of playing a guitar produced a change in the environment, i.e. a guitar goes out of tune with use, and tuning a guitar becomes part of what must be learned in order to continue to develop the guitar playing performance. Becoming aware that the guitar goes out of tune with use produced learning. New criteria emerged out of an interaction with her audience and created a change in her comparison of her performance to model performances. As Jessie learned to recognize the difference between in tune and out of tune she wanted a new thing, a guitar that was tuned, and this eventually led to a request for assistance, "Can you tune my guitar for me?" Jessie made a decision about her performance; a tuned guitar was now a conscious requirement for the performance and she is learning to recognize when it is out of tune. The ZPD now includes tuning a guitar, as an activity that cannot be completed without assistance. Her future development in the area of tuning her guitar and perhaps her ability to come to a more intimate relationship with the instrument may remain at the current level of development if she doesn't learn to tune the guitar herself. This will require more practice and experimentation on her part.

"Tool and Result"

Practicing tuning a guitar produces a tuned guitar and learning how to tune a guitar produces the practice of tuning a guitar. This dialectical relationship is referred to as "tool and result" in language used by Holzman and Newman to describe developmental learning (Newman and Holzman, 1993). More is possible for Jessie, her musical performance is still in its earliest stages of development, and the complex and demanding learning environment that she is immersed in will continue to change or increase in complexity as her learning and development continue. In the technology rich environment Jessie has created there is very little that is directly responsive (in person, in real time) to how Jessie is performing. Her online audience is appreciative and resources may unexpectedly become available, but she is lacking a more experienced performer who is providing direct guidance to how her performance is developing. Adding an experienced performer would create more complexity in the learning environment and more opportunities to create experiences that Jessie could not create on her own even with all of her technology and a supportive audience. For example, performing in a live duet or as part of a musical ensemble would be a developmental learning experience. If we view Jessie as a performer of a language called "playing the guitar" it becomes obvious that she doesn't have a live partner to speak that language with. Other performers must respond to her performance for her to learn to respond to the diversity and complexity that others can bring to ensemble interactions. Whether those performers are a teenaged rock band, or a private music teacher, Jessie will need more than she currently has if her performance is to continue to develop. If her father had not intervened, offered help that Jessie did not know that she needed, she might have continued playing a guitar that was increasingly out of tune.

Jessie's ZPD is what has been created with the artifacts and various social relationships she has available to her. She is actively making choices and taking risks and continuously evaluating how to proceed in performing for herself and her audience. If we are looking for a motive we can go back to the Vygotskian example of a language learner and see that "motivation" for becoming a speaker is not distinguishable from the human activity that produces a community of speakers. According to Holzman (2009, p 17) inserting the idea of "motivation" as something that is examined as part of the social activity eliminates the dialectical relationship in the methodological approach we are using. It's helpful to remember that babies don't have motives for learning language. Jessie is doing what other teens are doing and is interested in being part of a community of teens who perform music for an Internet audience. Guitar playing videos are part of the discourse in that community. Her family and friends value her guitar playing and are willing to offer direct support; she decides what offers she will accept.

Jessie has stated that learning is something that she does at school. She has developed a complex relationship to school learning that includes negative feelings when she is confronted with situations that make a lack of knowledge or understanding, a humiliating experience. Happily, Jessie, like many children and teens, continues to have opportunities to learn developmentally (playing on sports teams, pursuing her interests) outside of school even though she doesn't recognize that type of activity, pretending to be a music video star, as "tool and result" developmental learning.

Rubik's Cube on YouTube

I met a student in my first year of teaching middle school that had an IQ of 150. She was Asian, with long black hair and was 11 years old. She introduced herself by offering to recite PI out to 100 digits and to solve the Rubik's cube in less than two minutes. She eventually performed solving the Rubik's cube in the school talent show and we were all happy that she had chosen to participate in the school community in a new way. After one year she transferred out of the school into a specialized middle school for talented and gifted students. In my second year at this school I met several 6th graders who could also solve the Rubik's cube. In my third year there were even more new students who could solve the puzzle. Was the school attracting genius children?

I discovered that the students were accessing various YouTube videos on the Internet that provided algorithms (step by step instructions) for solving the puzzle. When the puzzle became popular in the 1980s it had taken me months to stumble upon a solution and I could not replicate my success. Now over 20 years later I was watching 11 year olds solve the puzzle in minutes and they had learned to do so by watching Internet videos produced by teenagers.

I attempted to learn to solve puzzle using the videos that my students recommended. I struggled to memorize the algorithms, and I could not invest the time that was necessary to do so. I was successful in learning to consistently solve two thirds of the puzzle, a big accomplishment for me, but solving the entire cube remained elusive. My students enjoyed finishing my cube for me and handing it back to me solved. This was more than mere rote memorization of the algorithm, they were able to recognize the current state of the cube and apply the appropriate steps in the algorithm. They were fluent in this algorithm.

The really interesting part for me in all this was that solving a Rubik's cube within minutes had become something that someone of ordinary intelligence could do with practice and good instructions. With the exception of the first student that I met who was identified as gifted, all of the others were students of average intelligence. The pedagogy for learning to solve the puzzle consisted of someone demonstrating the algorithm step by step, making a written code available for each step, and some tips for dealing with special cases. It was basically how we teach math. What was most interesting is that young people on the Internet had created a learning environment with an interest for sharing what they learned that was attractive to other young people. Technology was instrumental in their ability to share with peers and a general audience. Young people performing for an Internet audience are clearly performers of traditional approaches to learning delivered in a "cool" or engaging fashion with a music sound track. Young people are actively creating their own learning environments on the Internet and performance seems to be an inextricable part of what they are doing in their teaching and learning activities.

The Sports Talk Performance of a Teenaged Expert

Alex is 15 and attends a specialized New York City public high school. He is Latino, about 5'9" with a dark handsome face and hair cropped short. He lives in Section 8 public housing and goes to school with predominately Black and Latino students in Harlem, a neighborhood in Manhattan, in New

York City. Alex spends much of his free time playing video games and surfing the Internet on his computer. Those who know Alex also know that he is an expert in the area of Internet-based fantasy sports leagues and sports talk. Alex demonstrates knowledge of football, basketball and baseball statistics, betting odds, player contract negotiation strategies, sports economics, sports management strategies, public opinion, competitive match-ups and team dynamics. Alex's father, uncles, cousins and their friends regularly consult him on matters concerning their own fantasy sports league player draft strategies and team match-ups. His family encourages his interests and family gatherings usually include some sports talk with Alex in the middle of the conversation. Alex's father and uncles also take him to live sporting events on a regular basis.

Alex uses multiple sources for his information, he reads the newspaper, and watches news broadcasts on TV and visits sports websites on the Internet. He is also active on video game sports league simulations that use real world data as part of the interactive game play and strategy. This is in addition to many conversations with peers and adults who share his interests. He is immersed in a multimedia environment that is aligned with and designed to fuel his ongoing interests. His interests in sports talk and statistics emerged at about age 10. The collective movement of his family toward fantasy sports leagues coincided with the competence that Alex and his older brother demonstrated on the family laptop computer. Alex was able to provide his father with assistance and support in managing the Internet sites and accounts that they used to manage their fantasy sports team activities.

It's not clear whether Alex's interests translate directly into high academic achievement. Alex's middle school career had many ups and downs. He was fortunate to get into a small high school that focused on the business of sports. His performance in high school during his first year was erratic but ended in an A plus average, much to the surprise of his parents. Over time he has demonstrated an unwavering interest in pursuing a career in sports media. At the end of his first year in high school he secured an internship that had him attending basketball games to perform as a scorekeeper. His new performance as the recorder of raw statistical data provided him with new perspectives on the information that fuels sports talk. Like many teenagers his age, Alex's demonstration of expertise is not isolated to sports; he is also an expert in online warfare gaming and can provide detailed accounts of his use of various weapons and combat tactics that seem to be consistent with the best practices of combat soldiers.

Successful combat strategies and weapons specifications are designed into the gaming environments and therefore are part of the learning required for being successful at the games. The video games, the Internet-based fantasy sports software and the multimedia environments associated with those activities are designed as immersive environments that are competitive, collaborative and relevant to participant-audiences. There are millions of young people and adults who have integrated gaming and fantasy sports into the routines of their lives. They are no longer merely passive viewers of sporting events. The interactive participation in fantasy leagues changes how participants view the real sporting events they are based on. The line between the fantasies that we engage in using technology and the world that they are based on has become blurry. Alex is part of a generation of young people who are good at playing fantasy games that utilize massive amounts of information that is used to make choices or take action in a fantasy situation. The fantasy performances use real world information, this has implications for how Alex and his peers learn.

Design and Learning Principles

Video games and online fantasy sports simulations are designed learning environments that have certain learning principles built into them. James Gee (2003) identified 36 learning principles that are incorporated into the design of good video games and that have positive implications for literacy and good learning. A detailed review of those principles is beyond the scope of this book but a partial summary might highlight the significance of the multimedia environments that students are leaning in "on their own."

All of the learning environments examined so far are active and critical; they are designed to encourage active engagement through the use of a complex system of artifacts (words, images, symbols, sounds, devices) that are available or connected to affinity groups, i.e. musicians, an internet audience, fellow gamers, etc. Learning in a knowledge domain such as, music, football or warfare, is connected to other domains such as technology use, statistical analysis, and knowledge of historical events. Learners can take risks in these environments; consequences are limited to losing a game or having to do something over again. A high degree of commitment is observable on the part of the learners as they engage in the gaming, fantasy or performance activities. According to Gee learners can take on new identities. I would say that they are creating new performances. They are making choices based on the virtual performance or role that they have chosen or created.

In the video games, fantasy sports and online performances learners are rewarded for participation in the environment and their achievements are amplified (points for customization, leader boards, YouTube hits). Opportunities for feedback on performances are provided in different formats and may supply material for self-knowledge outside of a particular learning domain. For example, a fantasy sports gamer may discover he is good at remembering facts and details. In many successful gaming environments learners experience the feeling of being challenged to the edge of ability and opportunities for practice and tracking progress are easily accessible.

These designed learning environments provide an opportunity for the player to look ahead and make plans. For example, many fantasy football team owners check the fantasy league news to see if roster changes for next Sunday's match up are necessary based on injuries or recent performance history. As the learner becomes immersed in the performance of being the head coach or a video star, the things (artifacts, challenges, information) in the environment take on new meanings. As experience is gained situations that arise start to change or give shape to new perceptions. For example, a gamer may realize that he was shot the last time he was near a particular spot in a game and may learn to notice that there is a sniper on the roof by reflection of his sniper scope.

In the gaming, fantasy and performance environments initial success is critical. The learner starts out simply and basic skills are practiced. As the environments grow more complex, the learner is having success, experiencing pleasure, is doing more, and engaging more deeply. Skills continue to develop in the changing context and learners can be expected use higher order thinking skills. These skills include anticipating problems, and using different tools, such as pattern recognition, guessing, scenario building and model building in the course of play.

These types of environments tend to provide very little in the way of direct instruction, but information is made available on demand. For example, clicking a button to get an instructional video clip or a history of your performance with a particular weapon. Learners are expected to discover information and can be expected to juxtapose cultural models about the world into game play and models developed in game play into understanding the world. For example, getting killed in the game is easy regardless of skill, it is just as easy to get killed in real war, and you need lots of soldiers who will get killed to accomplish an objective. Similarly, on any given Sunday the underdog can win. The learner in the game, fantasy or performance realm is an insider and can make things happen in the learning environment. She or he distributes knowledge, creates it and makes use of it (creating music, putting together a team). The knowledge that is available in the learning environment can be found in the digital artifacts, technologies and other learners or participants in the environment.

People Create Learning Environments

Gee's learning principles are not confined to digital learning environments, an ensemble stage performance can embody all of those principles. A video game or a fantasy football league is an elaborate ensemble performance of "let's pretend" that allows the gamer to take part in and influence the performance. Just as young children engage in imaginative play, our Internet performing, cube solving, sports talking, young people can produce and program their own learning along the lines of their interests.

Designing these types of learning environments in our classrooms is within our ability. A helpful way of going about the design process is to turn classroom activities into games and projects that are relevant to students and take place in social contexts that they are interested in being a part of. The technology helps us to create those social contexts by providing students with the opportunity to contribute "a cool" way to do a math problem in a music video, or learning history by participating in a simulated historical game, i.e. "let's pretend we are George Washington and we have this challenge."

What I've discovered is that I do not have to provide all the knowledge and expertise necessary to design these types of environments. Some of the knowledge and expertise are embedded in the technology and media, and some of it is available in the social lives of the students. Students bring their own knowledge of media and culture to the learning environment and collectively they have a great deal of access to the different types of media and technology that are available on the Internet, communications devices and gaming devices.

In this chapter I have featured students who have demonstrated that they can create or access technology rich learning environments that embody the principles that Gee describes. If students are able to acquire practices, methods and facts from the Internet, of what use are textbooks and teachers? What do teachers do with students who have significant technical and content expertise on the first day of school? When I consider what I'd like to do with students in the classroom I imagine activities that might be engaging and relevant in that context. I start to think more like a corporate project manager with a staff of thirty than a teacher with a classroom full of kids. I look around at the available technologies and I think about what I am going to ask students to produce as evidence of their learning that contributes to the learning environment. I create a multi-step process so that there are several opportunities to give students feedback and provide guidance towards the development of end products. Multiple assessments are built into the process so that producing the end products is not something that can be left for a last minute attempt. I reduce the risk of failure by having checkpoints. For example, all student projects might be required to produce a plan and one or more milestone reports that identify challenges, report preliminary findings and provide status of tasks. I've also observed that the more connected the project theme is to the concerns, interests and passions of the students the more they invest. The challenge is in synthesizing a student's interest with the subject that I am responsible for teaching.

Structuring the activities so that they are rigorous and engaging is only the beginning of what I am doing. I am also trying to create an environment that is caring and demanding. The back and forth in my many relationships with students and between students is governed by the idea of creating a group that is inclusive and diverse. That's the one idea that I hold onto when the way forward seems unclear. It's within that context that I will change what I am doing and/or create an opportunity for someone else to do something new.

Project Based Learning

Access to the Internet and multimedia technologies is a critical part of the design of new learning environments in school because contact with the "real world" is possible. Opportunities to create "real world" content and "creative imitations" of the real world become available with technology. Creating a process for production and insuring that the tools for production are available and used effectively are part of trying to foster an environment that has high expectations and a high degree of communication among the students. I've used discussion forums, e-mail and messaging technologies to facilitate these types of interactions.

During my time in the classroom I relied on my professional management skills and my understanding of lesson and unit planning to produce classroom activities.

I've since discovered PBL or Project Based Learning tools that teachers may find helpful in designing classroom activities. PBL emphasizes learning through the process of producing a project. According to the PBL methodology, direct instruction is provided as needed during the project. PBL trainers point out that traditional approaches to classroom practice emphasize several lessons and then a culminating project activity to conclude the learning unit. The PBL approach stipulates that the project is the unit.

The performatory social therapeutic approach to teaching and learning that I have been presenting in these pages is NOT the same as PBL. Project based learning imposes a new framework, relevant and meaningful collaborative project work, on a traditional unit plan/lesson plan model. A performatory approach provides a methodology for creating learning environments that takes the history, culture, resources and the context of learners into account as part an ongoing effort to create development for communities and individuals by the activity of creating groups for learning and development.

HIGHLIGHTS

- In this chapter young people are featured as the creators of their own learning environments. They are depicted using multimedia technologies and performing in the context of complex social relationships that include friends, family and Internet audiences.
- The design principles articulated by James Gee are used to focus attention on how the technologies that young people use in their activities for play and fantasy align with these principles.
- The author briefly describes his process for creating classroom activities.
- A distinction is made between the PBL framework and the author's methodology.
- The "tool and result" dialectic is reflected upon as dynamic relationship describing the learner engaged in social activity.

QUESTIONS FOR DISCUSSION

1. Describe an instance where you were motivated to learn something outside of a formal learning environment. Did actual practices influence learning practices?
2. How do you go about creating an environment for your own learning?
3. What are your feelings on the multimedia learning practices of young people, what concerns or hopes are raised?
4. Do some research and identify one or more Internet sites or multimedia technologies that would provide an immersive experience for the subject that you teach. What would it take to make those resources available to your students?
5. Can you identify a dialectical relationship?

PRODUCING SCHOOL

During a question and answer session after a presentation of my "fantasy educational technology" a project I was presenting for a doctoral course I was taking, a dialogue resembling the following took place:

Setting: A graduate school classroom during student presentations. Jim is presenting and Tom is playing the Devil's advocate

Jim: What if we re-organized school as a multimedia production house, and the students produced the educational content? That content would be produced as digital texts, printed texts, audio and video performances. Students would contribute directly to the production process and teachers would be directors, editors and organizers of activity. Everyone's relationships to content and each other would change.

Tom: When would the students actually learn the content?

Jim: In the practice of producing it.

Tom: Wouldn't you still have to teach them some content using traditional methods?

Long pause

Jim: I didn't say we should replace the traditional methods. They already exist and that's what people know. I'm proposing that we allow other approaches to learning to exist side-by-side with traditional methods. That's what I meant by re-organizing.

Change Doesn't Deny What Came Before

Change is sometimes interpreted as the disappearance of what already exists in exchange for the presence of the thing that is new. We can find many examples of significant changes that did not result in the disappearance of what came before. Science did not eliminate religion and digital media has not replaced the book. The introduction of new paradigms or new technologies is part of the history of human beings engaged in the activity of creating culture. We make individual and collective choices about what must be done given the resources that are available to us. Along the way to change, access to different forms of power, political alliances, and control of resources may all shift in unpredictable ways.

What should teachers "teach" students to do in the midst a historical moment when everything is changing? How do we decide what content to teach when the content is being re-organized and created continuously? How can we move forward towards more developmental types of learning without leaving knowledge acquisition behind? In this chapter I attempt to lay out some of the pieces that I see in trying to put together a framework for a learning environment that is performatory, inclusive, relevant and responsive to the lives and concerns of teachers and students in 21st century schools.

Critical Pedagogy

There is a body of work devoted to the idea of a critical pedagogy. This is a pedagogy that examines how societal power relationships reproduce inequities and attempts to deconstruct or question the underlying beliefs, practices and assumption of those relationships in an educational context while empowering students to take ownership of their education (and political status) using various strategies. Paulo Freire is a central figure and contributor to the critical pedagogy literature and his approach was to use language literacy as a strategy towards liberation for oppressed people (Freire, 2003). Other ideas that run through the literature include, postmodernism, feminism, anti-racism, queer theory and decolonizing theories. The work of critical pedagogy is to produce positive change (equity, liberty, justice) for the poor and oppressed people of the world.

By the very nature of its focus on activity and participation, a performatory social therapeutic approach to teaching and learning advances the interests of a critical pedagogy. The methodology challenges existing habits of thought, ways of knowing, ways of being and meaning making that maintain the status quo. Why is this important?

Performatory social therapeutics is Newman and Holzman's synthesis of the works of Karl Marx, Vygotsky and Wittgenstein and is directly connected, through theorists and practitioners to grassroots efforts that have attempted and are attempting to effect positive change for poor, oppressed and forgotten people all over the world. For me, being reminded that I am contributing something that is much larger than my classroom and connected to efforts that are global in scale is helpful in providing a broader context for what I am doing when I am struggling with the ordinary events in my life.

I think it is also helpful to remind teachers who work in communities with high rates of poverty and illiteracy that the development of their teaching practices, requires that they question the efficacy of their practices. This is more than refining the use of teaching methods and existing classroom practices. Taking change seriously and committing to a critical teaching practice that has positive change and human development as a central concept, is hard work and encounters resistance in the bureaucracies that we teach in and in the minds of colleagues who would resist change in general and the disruptive change that critical pedagogies and technology facilitate in particular.

Teacher as Therapist – A New Role

Teacher as therapist means helping students develop as learners... (Holzman, 2009, p. 45).

Holzman is discussing the role of the teacher in the classroom from the vantage point of organizing the classroom as a performatory environment

...because it is performance that keeps us away from the paradigmatic dualism of cognition and emotion" (Holzman, 2009, p. 45).

She is advocating, viewing the learner in his or her entirety. The goal of the social therapist is to support people to create a therapy group, it is during the activity of creating the group that Newman and Holzman have discovered that people can get help with emotional pain (Holzman & Mendez, 2003). The social therapist tries to provide the group with a performatory direction.

It's in this context that I make sense of Holzman's "teacher as therapist." The teacher's task is to be the director of an ensemble performance where it is possible for students to learn and develop. Relating to individual performances, as something that happens in the context of an ensemble is a radical departure from seeing students as individuals that are assessed on their individual cognitive abilities. From the vantage point that Holzman suggests, the teacher takes on the task of creating the learning environment by directing performances and supporting the group. The directions that the teacher gives take many different forms but the intent is consistently on creating an environment where learning and development are possible in the context of the ensemble or community. I've discovered that my efforts in this direction may result in an environment that can be experienced or described as therapeutic. The following is provided to illustrate the point.

During my first class with a group of students in a teacher certification program, the psychology majors in the group, commented on how "therapeutic" the environment was. I had been actively creating the learning environment with them for the first 30 minutes or so that we had together. In doing so, I had addressed some of their initial concerns about being in a new class with a new professor. I relieved some of their anxiety about the course work and then pushed and encouraged them to participate more in the classroom discussion about the syllabus and what I meant by creating learning environments. I was slightly surprised by the comment, because it was the first time I'd ever used a performatory approach to learning with a group of adults in a college setting and I didn't have an awareness of how immediate the impact would be and how recognizable as therapeutic, the activity of being supportive was to psychology majors with no knowledge of Holzman, Newman, social therapy or Vygotsky. I was trying to be the director/producer getting performers ready for a fifteen-week performance. I wasn't trying to do therapy.

Learning How to Learn

The practical problem of being a teacher who uses technology is that the software and hardware that students are learning to use today will not be what they use in 5 years, in 36 months or even in 18 months. I've decided that teaching students that a spreadsheet is a tool that can be used to make other tools, such as graphs and budgets is a good use of the technology and the time invested. I don't spend much time on direct instruction with a large group. I allocate plenty of time for students to play around and practice with the technology. Students can play with pushing the different buttons to see what happens while trying to figure out how to create a budget for some project of interest. The practices of playing with different tools, using them in meaningful ways and being around others who are using similar tools are useful in preparing students to create or confront the next unimagined technology.

I believe that teachers should be teaching students how to learn, not just what to learn. I've come to recognize that learning must be a complex process that involves many different activities that take place in many different places in many different contexts among many different people. Learning inside of school impacts on learning outside of school even as learning outside of school impacts on learning in school. My practical experience in public schools has helped me to recognize that health, environment, nutrition, socio-economic status, race, ethnicity, gender and emotional well-being are relevant to learning in and out of school. These things constitute some of what there is and some of what is changing every time we enter a classroom or attempt to create a developmental learning environment. Technology, happens to make the circumstances that we teach in more complex, whether we like it or not. Access to Internet-based media, peers, outside experts and conflicting information on all manner of subjects create a new demand for increasing the sophistication of our approach to pedagogy. Becoming more sophisticated in our approach to pedagogy also involves becoming more public about our pedagogical choices and creating environments where teachers are not isolated or solely responsible for their students.

Knowledge is... a Commodity

I learned working for financial institutions that information and the knowledge that it comprises is a commodity that is of highest value when very few people have access. It decreases in value as more people have access to the information and the information becomes outdated. Textbooks are fairly expensive commodities that are outdated almost from the moment they are published. Publishers recognize this and have responded with electronic updates to their content via various storage media and Internet access for a subscription fee. In an environment where knowledge is not scarce and is being offered as a consumable product by a handful of national companies that seek to minimize customization with respect to regional and local curricular interests we are obligated to become critical of it and if necessary, create our own content.

School as Production House

I envision school as an organization that is concerned with it's own development in the context of the communities it exists in. Teachers might be directors, producers, and coaches of activities that were grounded in the interests of the learning community. School would become a place where students participated in the actual production of things that were important to the community. School newspapers, multimedia artifacts, books, performances, art exhibits and science projects that were focused on local concerns, would be produced in partnership with local institutions and interact with a potentially global audience. The following narrative about the development of my math video project illustrates an enactment of this concept.

Math Video Project

For a couple years we had been in a struggle with my daughter Jessie over helping her with math. It was very frustrating. She wouldn't let us help and she became very angry when the subject of her struggles with math came up. I was in grad school at the time and had been doing a lot of reading and studying on how performance transformed relationships and emotions. At around the same time I needed to put together a class project that used technology in a learning situation. I came to the conclusion that Jessie's "problem" was her relationship to math learning and getting help with it. If I could turn getting help with math into a performance it might transform her relationship and her emotions about what was going on. I decided to prototype the idea and submit it as a project proposal.

I recruited Jessie's cousin Alex who was in the seventh grade at the time to perform in a scene of tutoring Jessie who was in the sixth grade. They would be helping me with the class project by performing a tutoring session using a real math problem that Jessie was struggling with in school. We would use my laptop to record their performance and then I would upload the video recording to my Facebook account so that I could share it with my peers and professors.

The session was unscripted so I wasn't sure of what they would do, but they got really enthusiastic about it. Jessie combed her hair and put on lip-gloss and Alex practiced making sure he had a cool expression on his face as he checked himself out on the laptop display. They did the scene and it went beautifully, Alex helped Jessie with the math problem, she accepted the help without getting upset and they got to the right answer together. Throughout the recording they are performing the back and forth of a tutoring session and you can see that they are both aware of the camera. In the prototype you see them working and solving a problem and you see that they have positive emotions and are building a nice rapport. So the theory holds up, she actually did the math and had a totally different experience of getting help with it even though she struggled a little and even after Alex teased her. The idea of performing for an audience helped to produce that transformation. I submitted the prototype and I got a partner with a math background and identified an interested colleague who taught math and scaled the project up.

Brian was a math teacher at my school and he had asked me to do something with his class in terms of a technology integration project. He was interested in using video and had attempted a project on his own but had never gotten it off the ground. Now that I had a clear idea about what was possible I suggested some performance workshops and students producing their own videos. Brian's seventh graders had been my students as sixth graders and I knew that they had the technical competence and the resources at school to pull off their projects. We agreed that I would come in on Fridays and work with each of his classes taking half of the students for a half hour to work with them. He would work with the other half in small groups and then we would switch. The students were working for extra credit and were free to not participate. We did get a few students who initially opted out, but when they saw what everyone else was doing, some of them opted in. We worked together for about five weeks.

On the first day Brian reported that we had immediate dividends from the project, he told me that a couple of students had come back from the performance workshop and were excited about how they had performed their relationships to math in the workshop. We had played some improvisation games and I had asked the students to create some improvised scenes based on their feelings and attitudes about math. Brian said that he had been trying to find a way to approach these students all year and in that moment that they started sharing what they had done he saw a way to build the relationship.

Five weeks and a few dozen videos later, Brian and I debriefed. He reported several different transformations. Students had become enthusiastic about being in math class on Fridays and looked forward to working on their projects. In reviewing their video projects he was re-assessing how he was thinking about his students, one student who he thought was quiet in class because of shyness was singing on a video about being depressed about math. He realized that he needed to change his thinking about that student. He noticed the prevalence of humor in the videos. I guessed humor was important and surprising to him. He also saw clear evidence of student misconceptions about math in the videos, which he found interesting and useful. We also noticed that certain groups were working much harder than we expected on producing videos that looked good and were correct. I shared with Brian how I noticed that some students really struggled in talking about math during the improvised scenes that we did together. It was almost like they were trying to speak a foreign language where they knew some words, but were unable to express more complex concepts. Brian was definitely pleased with the results of the project and said he was inspired to try again and was interested in getting the students more focused on producing more of the kind of content he was looking for.

I was really pleased with the results as well but I had some doubts. The situation had been low risk and there were a lot of factors that were in my favor in this project. I had intimate knowledge of the setting, I had a lot of control over the technology resources and I was very confident that the students would perform to expectations. What if I didn't have all that control and access? Would students producing content be possible in other settings?

That remained an open question until several months later when I was sitting at lunch with Carol the CEO of a small non-profit that was facilitating an educational partnership program between schools in Detroit Michigan and South Africa. Carol and I had been friends for many years and she was interested in some of the work I had been doing with technology in education. I told her about my math videos project and she asked me to try the project with a school she was working with in Detroit. Here was my opportunity to see if using videos and the idea of performing for an audience was possible in a setting that I didn't control. It was also a worst-case scenario because we had almost no budget. We did have a couple of volunteers from corporations who were interested in working with the schools to help with the video recording using small digital video cameras. I volunteered my time and I took a trip to Detroit to meet with the volunteers and described the math video project to them. They liked the concept, but no one had any idea of how we could pull any of it off. I wound up on a couple of conference calls with the middle school math teachers that Carol recruited for the project. I also worked with her staff to produce a video where I explained to the students and their teachers how they could create a process to do math related projects. One suggestion I made was that they could use video technology to produce a video about their math projects. After they viewed the video that we sent I did a live videoconference with the students and teachers and they asked me questions. I did a follow-up telephone conference with the teachers a couple of weeks later to address some questions that they had. They reported that the projects were going well.

I didn't hear from the teachers again, Carol had been busy flying between Detroit and South Africa attending to other aspects of the partnership that she was responsible for. A couple of months later I reconnected with Carol and asked her about Detroit, she apologized and told me that the teachers had completed the projects with the students and that there had been a transformation. The teachers said that the project had been a positive new experience for them and the students said that they had a lot of fun doing their projects. Carol had spoken to the administrators and apparently the project was a big hit. She didn't have all the video in hand so I couldn't get more detailed information than that. I'm still waiting to get more information and to see some videos. I was a bit surprised that we had that kind of impact with such limited resources.

A few months after that I checked in with Brian and asked him if he was going to do a math video project again. He e-mailed me back and said that he had 80 videos, he asked every kid to make three and that he was applying for a grant. That was the cherry on the whipped cream topping. He changed his teaching practice even though he was on his own with his students. I came to conclusion that a math video project was methodologically sound within the framework I was proposing and it was scalable and sustainable.

The narrative serves to demonstrate my process for creating a project as well as illustrating a methodology that is performatory, improvisational and happens to use technology to create an environment where there is the possibility of an audience. It's important to note the students and teachers were participating voluntarily in new kinds of activity that were relevant to their interests. This included getting extra credit or integrating technology into teaching and was supported from outside of the institution. I came away from these projects with the sense that being able to make a change in a setting like a school was very difficult for individual teachers without outside support.

This is not a new idea, what was new was that the outside support, in the situations that I was a direct party to, was unconditional. The teachers were not required or coerced to work with me. I had something to offer and others were prepared to accept my offer. They were also not asked to do anything that they didn't already know how to do on their own. Volunteers and students supported the new technologies and they helped in creating ZPDs. The only thing that teachers had to do was be receptive to what the students were doing, given that everyone had agreed to give the projects a try.

There are no improved test scores to point to. There is no claim that we increased student attendance. These are important things, but it was not the focus of my participation with the students and teachers. Teachers reported higher levels of enthusiasm and engagement. Students reported that they enjoyed the activities and produced tangible evidence of their process and products in the form of digital video. The projects gave teachers new ways to relate to students and provided students with a new means to express their understandings of the content. There is also evidence that one teacher, myself not included, undertook a significant change in his teaching practices. All of this was accomplished with little or no money, the existing technology and just some time and effort on the part of interested adults and enthusiastic students.

Making performance a self-conscious component in a learning activity constitutes a significant change in pedagogical approach. In traditional acquisition learning pedagogy we talk about and read about what we are learning and the goal is to *know about things before* we attempt to do (experience) things. The result, in my opinion, is that the ability to respond without *knowing* is underdeveloped and so we do not attempt new things and we do not make choices and we do not respond well to change. What I've learned in many conversations with Holzman, and others, is that what seems to get lost in traditional approaches to learning content is developing the capacity of the student to learn content.

Observation and Reflection

What I've gathered from my reading is that the knowledge acquisition approach to learning and the exclusive focus on individuals and their ability to acquire knowledge is limiting of human creativity and development (Newman & Holzman, 1997). During my career in information technology I often collaborated with others on project teams to create new systems, things that did not already exist except in our minds and project plans. It's both exciting and daunting to be in a creative moment with other people. These types of experiences can also be had in art, dance, sports and music. When artists collaborate together they don't know what they will produce together until they've produced it. Whether we are technology professionals or artists at some point in our work we go beyond what we know in the process of becoming creative or in responding to unique circumstances.

Collaborative group work produces different demands on all the people involved. Risk-taking, struggle and anxiety are produced and the teacher has to be involved in the learning environment as a creative director of the group's performance (Holzman, 2009). Problem solving and negotiating become the activities that students and teachers are engaged in as an ongoing part of the collaborative process. Zones of proximal development emerge continuously during a group's activity as different skills are required and different aptitudes are brought to bear by group members.

Students (and teachers) who are resistant to working in collaborative groups need time, opportunities and support to get used to working in that environment. I've observed that good teachers routinely observe student development throughout course the school year, they are not only looking in the area of skill and knowledge acquisition. They are looking at social skills, relationship development, emotional development, and even physical development. The totality of a student's well-being and development is of interest to good teachers.

In my experience reflections on observations of students and teaching practices are typically problem focused. We are asked to use our observations to provide causal explanations for the problems that students have in school. In a problem-solving context it is difficult to use a reflection for anything other than rationalizing a deficit perspective. The process establishes deficits, i.e. "Johnny lacks the following skills and knowledge…" and then proceeds to provide resources to address the deficit.

A process that used student observations and teacher reflections in a non-deficit perspective would continuously create development, in the form of new projects, activities and opportunities to collaborate. Observations and reflections become the material to build new performances with. Based on my own experiences, I would argue for the need to support learning new ways to be reflective from outside of the traditional schooling framework. My experience with my doctoral studies and with the Institute made it clear to me that there are many different resources outside of school with expertise in reflective practices.

In this chapter I've described my "fantasy educational framework" which is designed from a performatory social therapeutic perspective. This perspective directly challenges the individualized deficit perspective of traditional interventions and offers creative alternatives that feature group work, performance, and outside expertise to support transformations with respect to content learning and pedagogy. This chapter is my extended response to the "Devil's advocate" who is challenging what may be at first glance a proposal to eliminate school in it's current form and replace it with something that might be construed as less rigorous.

HIGHLIGHTS

- The author lays out his argument for re-imagining schools as production houses with teachers and students taking responsibility for producing content and knowledge that is relevant to their lives.
- A narrative of the author's experience in developing an approach to integrating technology in the mathematics content area is provided as a proof of concept.
- The author proposes an alternative to deficit perspectives in observations and reflections.

QUESTIONS FOR DISCUSSION

1. How is creating school as a site of production as the author describes it within the community different than what we normally do at school?
2. How do you think people with privilege and resources think about change and what needs to change?
3. How would you challenge this chapter as the "Devil's Advocate?"
4. What do you think is the author's stance on knowing and knowledge acquisition learning?
5. How do you feel about the author's stance on knowing and knowledge acquisition learning?
6. How do you use your observations and reflections?

BUILDING RELATIONSHIPS

The Hacker

Aaron was an eighth grader the year I started working at Manhattan Middle School. I became aware of him when he joined a computer programming oriented elective that I was teaching that included 6th, 7th and 8th grade students. Aaron was thirteen and he had dark hair, pale skin, and an average build for a boy his age. He wore black t-shirts, jeans and had braces. He was interested in computer hacking and security. Aaron seemed very bright and motivated, he considered himself a "white hat" or good guy type of hacker.

The elective was 6-weeks long and ended early in the spring semester but Aaron didn't let our ongoing conversation about computers and hacking stop there. He began to follow me in the hallways between classes and during lunch breaks so that we could talk. Aaron's story began to emerge as I began to ask the 8th grade teachers and the guidance counselor about our resident hacker. It turned out that they all viewed Aaron as an indifferent student in their classes. He failed to hand in homework and project assignments. According to them, he was jeopardizing his chances for getting into a good high school. His teachers expressed their frustration with him and it seemed that at least some of his problems were attributed to issues in the home. A couple of teachers had noted that he appeared quite taken with me and urged me to encourage him to work harder or to take the schoolwork seriously. I was shocked to find out that Aaron had these "problems." The "problems" didn't seem to get in the way of him learning about computers in the way that they did with schoolwork, if what everyone said was true.

When Aaron and I discussed computers his face lit up with excitement and passion, he demonstrated knowledge and skills that indicated many hours of commitment. When I conveyed my views to the other teachers they pointed out that the computer activity was coming at the expense of the schoolwork. My first impulse was to not involve myself with what anyone else wanted Aaron to do. I viewed my relationship with Aaron as a new kind of performance for us and I found our conversations delightful. I was not operating from within a tightly constrained teacher role, he was not "my student" and I was not grading him.

Even though we were not in a traditional student-teacher relationship, it was important to me that Aaron understood certain concepts and that he understood that there was a body of work in computer science that he could make better use of. We would laugh when I pointed out that he couldn't solve or understand particular problems because of gaping holes in his knowledge of facts or computer programming theory. He would go away and come back having studied on what I pointed out and would begin to pepper me with questions. We were having a good time, I felt like I was giving him something he wanted and I felt energized when he gave me his questions and his enthusiasm. I was happy with our informal arrangement and I didn't want to ruin it by pushing him to do schoolwork and yet I didn't want him to fail or miss out on opportunities.

Aaron's computer hacking activity had led him to start asking questions about, ethics, property, the law and the exercise of authority and personal freedoms. He began to ask for my opinions on these subjects and over time our conversations became broader. I began illustrating my perspectives with examples from my personal life and my political views on the role of technology in culture. Aaron also started to share some of the difficulties he was having with his parents and his ambition to start making money as a computer security consultant.

I eventually decided to share my dilemma with Aaron. I told him what I knew about his academic situation and he confirmed it and shrugged, he just wasn't interested in what was being offered in his courses. He said that he really couldn't see the point of any of it. I made it clear that I was sympathetic to his position. I responded by sharing my reasons for having a career in education and how I wanted to change the way that schools did things. I started to "unpack" with him, what I saw as difficulties that were being created at school for him and many other students. Over the course of several conversations I pointed out the gaps in his general understandings of math, science and social studies as they related to his broader questions. I then proceeded to help him see the relationships between his interests and the various subject areas that he had dismissed as irrelevant.

Aaron eventually pulled his academic situation together to a sufficient degree to satisfy his teachers, the guidance counselor and his parents. At graduation Aaron's parents thanked me for helping Aaron so much. Aaron got into a good high school and he occasionally visited or e-mailed me. We also became friends on Facebook. In my most recent communication with Aaron he indicated that (at age 16) he was involved in a start up Internet marketing company.

Changing Totalities

I take Aaron's parents seriously when they say that I helped their son. It's impossible for me to point to the one thing that made a difference for Aaron. The totality of his relationship to schooling changed and I had been part of that totality. Aaron's parents acknowledged or verified that Aaron was helped and they perceived a causal relationship that they singled out amidst all of the other kinds of helping relationships that were available. Our relationship opened up the possibility of Aaron making better use of the resources available to him, even though that was never the specific purpose of our relationship.

Aaron developed cognitively and emotionally. He was helped to make connections between school subjects and an activity that he was passionate about. Aaron and I also created an environment where he was supported to take responsibility for his relationships to schoolwork and teachers. Holzman's understanding of the zone of emotional development (ZED) is that it is the ZPD of emotions (Holzman, 2009). This understanding comes from her experience of what happens in the practice of social therapy (Holzman & Mendez, 2003). According to Holzman, people creatively and collectively working together in social therapy create an "emotional zone" that creates a new emotionality (Holzman, 2009). Our activity (conversations) created a ZED that provided an environment where tools were made (historical, socio-cultural, and emotive-cognitive understandings and artifacts) that Aaron could use to dialectically transform his situation.

Our relationship transformed who we were to each other and as our conversations unfolded our concerns and interests changed. New wants and needs were created for both of us. My "improvised" teaching included bringing in things that I knew about technology, philosophizing and creating a dialogue that was focused on what we were interested in, not on finding a solution to the "problems" that Aaron and I had in school. By including my motives, feelings, and dilemmas as part of the conversation I was able to create, with Aaron's help, a way I could make my views, concerns, and opinions available with out being coercive or compromising the integrity (trust) of our relationship. In other words, I was able to take responsibility for our relationship (teacher/student, friends, master/apprentice) and provide some leadership, by talking about what was going on and making my concerns available to Aaron as I related to him as the young adult he was in the process of becoming. Subsequently, Aaron took responsibility for what he needed to do and provided his own leadership to his interactions with others. Aaron's activity was to engage in a positive relationship with an adult with common interests. He acknowledged a situation that was problematic for him and he was supported to make a series of choices and decisions. He was able to change the totality of what was happening to him.

Aaron's story exemplifies a relationship that develops as it comes in to social contact with various cultural institutions. Upon reflection, I see that our relationship and our group included other teachers, Aaron's parents, students and other people in our lives who were influencing us, whether we were conscious of it or not. As the school community began to acknowledge, comment, and enter into conversations with each of us, ideas, comments, information, opinions and agendas of others, were provided. Our conversations changed as we were impacted by what went on around us. I learned to view input from others as a type of performance direction that I was free to accept or ignore without judging. Our relationship resonated positively with the school community and the parents and so they supported it and provided both direction and affirmation.

In our created learning environment we were happy to talk about the "subject." Learning included, talking, reading, and doing activities. This produced more enthusiasm and happiness. We had produced a flow experience, teaching and learning for us had become optimal (Csikszentmihalyi, 1990). It was literally something that we did as we walked along together, losing ourselves in talk in the heart Manhattan's busy streets. As our relationship developed I was able to help re-contextualize the "school subjects" in a way that didn't disrupt the flow of the conversation. We had successfully produced a Wittgensteinian "vanishing of" the problems of Aaron "the problem student" and school as "a waste of Aaron's time." What we created for Aaron was an opportunity to develop his capacity to learn, to take responsibility for the demands being placed on him, even as my presence in a relationship with him created a new perspective on Aaron for others. Others, including his parents, teachers and administrators were reassured when an adult took responsibility for the problem of Aaron's "indifference" to schoolwork.

Something new happened at school, learning for Aaron became a social, "tool and result" activity (Newman & Holzman, 1993, 1997). Aaron learned something about learning at school as it related to his learning in the pursuit of his interests. Learning was no longer limited to an instrumental "tool for result" activity that had to meet Aaron's criteria (or an institutional criteria) in order to be considered relevant. Aaron's activity at school changed from a traditional view of school, i.e. "it's not relevant to my interests," to something like, "I need some knowledge to pursue my interests and school may be able to fill the gaps, but I have to work at it."

A Problem Pair

When Will and Robin were in the 6th grade their teachers identified them as best friends who should not be allowed to work on projects together. According to their teachers they were both capable of doing the work but together they seemed to be unable to complete projects. The boys were not hostile towards their teachers, nor were they indifferent. They simply wore grins on their faces as if they were sharing an inside joke and publicly acknowledged their many failings as students. For most of the school year I aligned my practices with those of my colleagues and kept them apart on projects. When they proposed working together for the final project I was not happy about the proposal and I encouraged them to seek other partners. They were insistent and I relented. I made it clear that we were all taking a high stakes gamble, the final project was a significant portion of their grade and I didn't want to be placed in the position of failing them because I decided to go against the conventional wisdom.

The final project was a complicated project that involved writing a proposal, developing a plan of action, obtaining my approval for the project and then producing the project. There was also a reflection piece at the end of the project that detailed the experience and what they believed they had learned. The final project was open ended; the students could select any technology and any topic, and needed to submit a final product, some digital artifact that they created. The proposal, plan and reflection needed to be posted on a Wiki page that I had set up for the students. I would use the Wiki to post my approval and my feedback and suggestions for their proposals. We would also use the Wiki to update the status of their projects.

They settled on a Microsoft MovieMaker animation. The animation was no more sophisticated than stick figures drawn with Microsoft Paint and the boys did not demonstrate much in the way of design or artistic creativity, so it wasn't very attractive, but I considered it to be the beginning of a very innovative effort. Midway through project they became dissatisfied with the quality of the work and switched production to a personal laptop that contained Apple's iMovie. They were able to improve the quality of the production and finished on time. When they completed their project they had neglected to update the Wiki to provide the reflection on the project that I had asked for. Not providing a reflection would result in an incomplete project. I reminded the boys and provided a time extension to finish up the documentation. A week later, the reflections were not yet done. Frustrated, I asked the boys what the collective problem was. They indicated that they just didn't want to sit down to write everything up. All sorts of things flashed through my mind at this point, everything from thinking them lazy to considering the futility of asking boys this age to write anything without the threat of dire consequences.

I thought about what I really needed from them, I needed to know that they could somehow share what they had learned in the process. I realized that being able to talk to them about their work would be more than adequate as a substitute for having them write about their work. I asked them if they would each agree to be interviewed by me so that I could "type up" their reflections on the Wiki page. They both agreed and I was able to interview and assess their learning to my satisfaction, the assignment was completed and their team received an A on the project. In their reflections they mentioned things like "We achieved more than I expected." And "we took this a lot more seriously and wanted to make up for the beginning of the year, we just cut out the fooling around."

Two years following that project Will recalled in a conversation with me that he had gotten an "A" on the project and expressed his amazement at the fact that he and his partner had done something that was not very pretty and had been "rewarded" anyway. I reminded Will that he and his partner had done the work I had asked for, had been fairly clever, and had completed the project. As eighth and ninth grade students Will and Robin were separated in the classroom but each in his own way continued to resist what teachers were asking them to do. While I was never in a position to work with them again in my capacity as "classroom teacher," I would characterize our interactions as warm and playful, and when the need arose I could ask them to be more "respectful" if the occasion required me to ask it of them.

Will and Robin saw an opportunity to work together and to work on a project that they were interested in doing and they made a decision to stop "fooling around." It's unclear what prompted that decision. Maybe we can take them at their word and it was a "make up for the beginning" kind of effort. It's clear that they were working in a classroom environment where making up for a poor start was possible. My policy was always to weigh the final project more heavily than the preceding projects. Students understood that I wanted creative, over the top projects that demonstrated that they could integrate multiple technologies into a coherent digital artifact. Students who struggled early usually had "aha" moments late in the school year. I also think that some students simply need more time to figure out how to be a 6th grader and complete a major project. It was in this environment, that Will and Robin made their final push and learned something about collaborating and integrating technologies. I've never understood why some teachers insist on weighing grades at the beginning of the year equally with grades at the end, learning is not a linear process!

A NASA Flight Operations Controller

Steve introduced himself as a future NASA space flight operations controller in the first PowerPoint presentation that his 6th grade class was assigned. There were pictures downloaded from the NASA website that showed rockets, space shuttles, planets and stars. He was very articulate in all things related to NASA and it was clear that his family supported his interests as he indicated that he had attended space shuttle launches at the Kennedy Space Center, in Cape Canaveral, Florida. Steve talked about his passion for NASA, technology and the related sciences incessantly. He tended to dominate conversations and was slightly insensitive to listeners who did not share his passions. He enjoyed technology class and was always eager to do a little more than was necessary or expected. For example, one day he came in excited about a shuttle launch that was scheduled to happen at the same time that I was teaching his class and he asked if we could set up a live Internet video stream into the classroom. I allowed him to set up the equipment to do so while I carried on with my lesson and we stopped to watch when the video stream was ready.

Steve surprised me one day when he had decided not to do a PowerPoint presentation for a cross-curricular project about ancient Egypt. I pursued the matter with him, I had to give him a grade for the assignment and he had nothing for me. That didn't stop him from trying to engage me in a conversation about a robotics project he was interested in doing for Tech Class. I left that conversation with the understanding that he would do the Egypt project and then I spoke to his humanities teacher. Steve had completed the humanities portion of his Egypt project, but he didn't seem to have much interest in it. When I followed up with Steve, he presented me with a very minimal effort, far below what he was capable of. It looked like he'd only spent a few minutes working on it. I said as much to Steve and he said, "I know." I asked him what was going on with this project and he said, "I'm not interested." I said that I couldn't give him a very good grade for it and he shrugged and said that he was fine with it.

As I grew to know Steve over the next two years I saw that he never deviated from his path to NASA. Everything seemed focused on that single goal. He did well in math and he complained loudly to his science teachers about the lack of time spent on planetary science and physics. Steve would seek me out around the school, asking me questions about computer technology and sharing his various interests in computers, robotics, ham radio, NASA, photography and classic rock.

Let's Make a Deal

Elena was very intelligent and seemed very quiet. She was Asian and had long straight black hair that she wore in a braid down her back to her waist. When I had opportunities to talk to her she displayed a sarcastic wit and considerable impatience toward her peers. Some time during the second half of the school year she started to struggle. I had noticed when I checked in on her that she had not even begun the project we were working on and was not interested in starting it. When I confronted her about it, she politely and firmly let me know that she had more important work to do. I was a bit taken aback, but I admired how she was being so straightforward with me, no lies, no excuses, my assignment just wasn't a priority for her. She looked tired and she quietly complained of being tired. We talked about how she would make use of her time in my class. I discovered that she was doing work for other classes in my class. I was still interested in seeing her complete her next project for me so we made a deal. As soon as she could make my project a priority she would complete the project and hand it in. Until then, during our class time she would do work that could be done on a computer so that she wouldn't be seen as just sitting and reading. Elena kept her deal with me and she went on to do well in my class and in all her other classes.

Let's Not Escalate

My desire not to coerce or punish students influenced my interactions with Elena, Steve, Aaron, Will and Robin. I didn't want to make their problems any bigger. What was being offered to me, were problems that had more to do with their inability to confront situations that were a bit "taller" than they were, outside of their ZPDs. Experienced teachers will recognize that I had many tools at my disposal. I could have ignored the rationalizations and made phone calls, insisted that certain conditions be met, withheld having a personal connection, or I could have tried various other sticks and carrots to bring them into line. Instead, I took the opportunity to try some creative things with some students who presented these unusual opportunities.

Jim's Tech Class Revisited

These students, each in their own way, provided what I took to be a critique of schooling. From their perspectives school priorities didn't match up with their priorities. In an environment where they were not being coerced, they gave expression to that. Aaron and Steve had passions for subjects that they felt were not being directly supported in school. Will and Robin didn't fit in, they knew it, and took on the roles of outsiders or class clowns. Elena precisely articulated that her priorities were school subjects that mattered. In the learning environments that I attempted to create with all of the students, I related to them as the adults they would one day be, I was trying to get them to move forward without trying to convince them that something was important even though they thought otherwise.

Aaron's interests were given a new context, Steve and Elena negotiated for terms we could live with and Will and Robin were transformed into students who could get a project completed, with a little support, much to their surprise. I call the ZPD/ZED that we performed in, creating the learning environment known as Jim's Tech Class. We were all part of interrelated interactions that were being produced at different points in time that influenced our ways of being together. Jim's Tech Class developed over the course of the 7 years that I taught in public schools and the events described here overlapped with each other and many other events that I was a party to with hundreds of other students. My decisions were not just momentary, improvised whims; they were part of my history as an educator, a business professional, a student, and a parent. When I decided to "deal with" my students improvisationally there was a great deal of experience, knowledge and structure in working with other people that was being called upon.

The skeptical reader may dismiss these happenings as insignificant and perhaps they are. Students did not do the things that they were supposed to do when they were supposed to do them and nothing of great significance happened. I am fairly certain that the skeptical reader would not automatically "buy" the argument that what I created with these students was a more demanding environment that was more humane than the schooling environment that normally gets created. To those who are skeptical I offer the following:

- Aaron's parent's and other teachers said I had positive impact on his school performance even though I was never his classroom teacher.
- Steve moved from refusal to cooperation in doing something that he deemed unimportant with out being disrespectful or being disrespected. He also took responsibility for a decision about a task that was not critical to his mission and accepted the consequences. A good quality in a flight controller.
- Robin and Will got to work together and they completed a project, something that had not been done on previous attempts and that no one believed they could do.
- Elena was able to be honest about her priorities and those priorities were respected and she was faithful to her agreement to complete the required work at a later time.

These "outcomes," were observable and demonstrated student knowledge and critical thinking (making choices). Students participated in decisions regarding their education and they were expected to follow through on commitments. They were respected and supported as diverse individuals with diverse interests. These are a few possible "outcomes" of the hundreds of stories I could tell about my students and the learning environments they helped to create.

Failure

I learn more from my failures with students than my successes and I am always willing to risk creating new failures. What I've learned about my failures with students was that I played a significant role in creating those failures. I had to share those failures with people who were outside of schools so that I could reflect on them without subjecting myself to the incessant "you should listen to me" type of negative criticism and advice that is typically available to novice teachers. During the course of my teaching career I have increasingly relied on support from my colleagues outside of the school system. My failures were related to as scenes in my life that could be learned from and performed differently. There was no particular outcome that we were trying to achieve with the new performance. The challenge was to produce a new performance! I approach the possibility of my students' failures from the same perspective; the only difference is that they didn't have to go outside of school to gain my support.

Different Kind of Teacher

I am interested in working with others to develop cognitively, emotionally and socially. To create that environment, I organize groups of students to work together. Their many interactions produce valuable learning experiences and resources in the classroom. The students featured in this chapter separated themselves from their peers in particular ways and so I found myself coaching and mentoring during my interactions with them in and outside of the classroom.

My focus was to discover what they were willing to do, or at least to get them to articulate what the difficulty was. Once we moved to that point, it was relatively easy for me move the seemingly immovable obstacles or unchangeable conditions (due dates, the assignment, an expectation). When most students that I've worked with see that I am seriously taking action on their concerns, they become more flexible, more willing to try and most importantly, they relax and start to make progress on the work. My "different kind of teacher" performance can trigger a different kind of student performance and that's when everything is transformed. In my experience students don't always acknowledge or provide evidence that they are aware that something different is going on when I am doing my "different kind of teacher" performance. That doesn't mean that they don't notice, or that something hasn't changed for them, it means that there is nothing I could detect as different on the student's part.

Focus on the Group

We spend enormous amounts of time and energy designing interventions for individuals in schools. The majority of the students in groups I've supported want the freedom, opportunities and responsibilities being offered in my classroom. That's possible when I focus on groups. Groups have a great deal of influence on individuals, and, as noted by Newman, very little patience with individuals who want to dominate what the group is doing (Holzman & Mendez, 2003). Groups help me create an environment where everyone is working on something with someone. Casting the teacher-student relationship in this context allows me to be more creative in my interactions and creates a broader range of opportunities for individuals in the group.

Why Relationships?

Information and communication technology, when used in the classroom, can provide a high level of interaction with students both in terms of quantity and quality. What do you do with all the interactions that are possible? Unless we develop new approaches to teacher-student interactions we will simply reproduce the interactions that we already understand and that fall short of being supportive of developmental learning. In a ZPD learning happens amidst social interactions with experienced others who relate to the less experienced members of the group ahead of their current level of development. In a classroom where most if not all of the learners are inexperienced and the teacher is most experienced person in the group, a performatory approach to learning is very challenging. It's challenging because there is only one person who has skills and the experience that are needed to learn the curriculum. That is why I believe that using technology and the Internet are so critical to the learning environments that I am creating with students. The technology can be used to create opportunities for students to bring diverse interests, and distribute knowledge and experiences in the classroom. With technology diverse learners have multiple avenues to content and can experience a richer curriculum via a multimedia environment. Diverse rates of learning can become a resource for supporting the development of the entire group if developing helping and collaborative relationships are a central focus.

HIGHLIGHTS

– A variety of relationships in the school setting are showcased to illustrate different approaches to working with students.
– Supporting student choice making brings the to the forefront the coercive nature of schoolwork.
– Qualitative outcomes of student-teacher interactions are listed.
– The author's approach to failure is presented.

QUESTIONS FOR DISCUSSION

1. Can you describe your relationships to students you find difficult?
2. Can you describe your relationships to students you enjoy working with?
3. How would you describe the language and tone you take with students?
4. What are your feelings about rules and deadlines with students?
5. How would you describe the difference between being demanding and be coercive?
6. What is your relationship to failure?

TEACHER PREPARATION

In the spring semester following my graduation from the CUNY Graduate Center I had the opportunity to start working with college students. It had been nearly ten years since I had worked with college students as an adjunct professor in a computer science course. This opportunity was ideal, the course was titled Elementary Instructional Technology and I felt well qualified to teach it even though I did not have much of an opportunity to prepare for it. I was filling in for the person who was supposed to fill in for a professor on sabbatical.

During my first class with the students I noticed there was a similarity in their responses questions to those of 6th graders. They were unwilling to respond to open-ended questions. These students were enrolled in a teacher preparation certification program in New Jersey, some of them already had undergraduate degrees and some were in the process of finishing one up. It made perfect sense to me that they would be more comfortable answering questions they knew the answers to. Their responses were ingrained and automatic, twelve successful years of schooling plus college had worked to insure certain responses. While I don't think that they appreciated being compared to sixth graders I used that as an example to illustrate the extent to which we are trained to respond in certain ways to certain situations in a school setting. Adult learners are nothing like the young learners that they once were. In my view, there is no reason for them to continue responding to what goes on in a learning environment in the same way that an adolescent would.

As the weeks progressed we got into our work together and my students read early versions of the first four chapters of this book and provided useful feedback as they learned about me, Holzman and Newman, Vygotsky, and the performatory approach to integrating technology into the learning environment that I have discussed throughout this book. They immediately grasped that I was working with them in a way that was outside of the norm but they seemed willing to go with what I was doing. As we established our routines and I communicated my expectations they started to respond by taking more risks and talking more in the classroom. I taught them some improvisation games, which proved to be very useful when they refused to respond during group discussions that forced them to venture out of their comfort zones (knowing the answer) and into the discussions we were trying to create.

We used the games to create a shared experience; they created a little discomfort, but they also generated giggles and laughter. Somehow that shared experience created the possibility of participating in conversations without being totally sure of what you were saying or sure that your response was correct. Having that shared experience created an environment were I could playfully and seriously point at a student, say, "we are playing a game" and say, "give me a one word response" and move around the room so that we could generate some responses to work with. We played that little game a couple of times. I never used it as a way to generate a correct answer, which would have produced negative feelings or unnecessary anxiety. I used that game, to initiate a conversation in response to an open ended question with no obvious correct answers. Those questions were part of the game that I played with them throughout the semester.

FINAL REFLECTIONS

Toward the final weeks of the semester I pushed harder for the group to take over the discussion and make better use of my knowledge and experience. This was the most challenging thing that I tried to do with them. There were occasions when there was uncomfortable silence in the room when I refused to make things easy by lecturing at them while they sat and took notes. During the final weeks of the semester things started to change for them as I tried to have them take more responsibility for what went on in the classroom. They all started coming into class stressed and less prepared. They were all trying to finish papers and prepare for finals and were trying to be efficient with the amount of effort they put out for any single class. Since we were a small group with only eight students I had been able to provide a great deal of individual feed back during the course of the semester and I had given them the opportunity to submit first draft assignments for feedback and revision before submission for a final grade. I'm sure they were feeling confident that I would give them good grades. In my experience as a student I gave more effort and attention to the courses that I struggled in, not the courses that I enjoyed or felt comfortable in, those always seemed easier.

I developed an assignment that made use of their weekly reflections papers as the material for a final paper we called an investigation. It was to be an investigation of their learning over the course of the semester and I used the way I was writing this book as a model for them. I also suggested that their thoughts and work might be an interesting and valuable contribution to the book. This chapter is that contribution so what follows is some of what my students created in our class. Hopefully you will see the diversity of understandings that students came away with in their concrete examples of what can be accomplished in creative collaborations with children. I'm very proud of their work; I was moved by their willingness to share their stories and to struggle in the learning environment that we created. They demonstrated that they were willing, in an environment that deliberately created a sense of playfulness, to attend to how they felt about their situations and to take the risk of trying something new. What follows is a brief summary of their reflections

Reflections

Since it appears that the use of technology permeates our world, how would this practice find its place in a setting where some feel that textbooks and the experts (teachers) rule the domain of educating students? Before this class, I

pondered about the following: "What are the effects of using technology in the classroom? As a future educator, how can I use technology as an effective means of engaging students in their lessons?" "Are there other methods of creating an optimal learning experience?" Over the past couple of months, our class explored these notions and I must say that I feel that I have gained an insight or rather enlightenment. Through various exercises and readings, it is clear that technology can really have a purpose in the classroom as a means of creating an environment where students can creatively voice their ideas and connect to others. In addition, there are various methods that can assist students to reach beyond their scope and aid them to a better understanding of their lessons. - Kate

Lindsey shared that she had a student who was ahead of others in a classroom activity and that he was sitting near a student who was struggling. The student had completed the activity and asked if he could work with his struggling classmate. She didn't hesitate to grant permission and the struggling student was able to complete his assignment with the assistance of his peer and he was quite proud of the accomplishment. Lindsey experienced this as a moment she would always remember. She said *"If students are treated like they are part of the learning process they will be more eager to participate, and in this case even assist other students"* she felt that it was an *"illustration of Vygotsky's theory of proximal development at work!"*

Anna felt that *"Being able to create an environment where students are comfortable asking for help when needed, but also where they can have free reign to work independently is crucial"* She believed that an effective teacher can combine both working collaboratively with working independently.

Suzy stated *"...allowing that student to lead an improv game, or lead a discussion in a classroom, or work with new technology in the classroom may place that student 'a head taller.'"* According to her this constituted a new result for the student.

Alan claimed that his attitude toward teaching had been transformed during our course.

DISCUSSION OF PROJECTS

Tutoring

Lindsey's project was very simple and straightforward; she decided to tutor a 4th grader. The 4th grader had no prior experience in creating PowerPoint presentations. Lindsey's focus was to make the presentation an art appreciation project. The student's task was to locate art on the Internet and then comment on the pieces that he found in the PowerPoint presentation. In this one-on-one setting Lindsey, the more capable or experienced adult, described sitting side-by-side with the child at the keyboard and demonstrating opening up the PowerPoint application and creating the first slide. She also demonstrated going out onto the Internet and putting a picture into the PowerPoint slide and creating some text. That was the extent of her instruction. She remained by the child's side at the keyboard while he attempted and achieved success at creating his own new slides. He created the slides and located the pictures through Google searches using various keywords that she had provided. He was able to create a PowerPoint presentation with several slides, each slide had color and was illustrated by the picture that he found and contained his comments on his experience of the pictures. He acquired vocabulary for some of his comments in his conversation with Lindsey about the pictures he selected for his presentation. He spoke about what he liked in each of the pictures that he selected. In her presentation Lindsey discussed that she felt he had really been able to take over the activity very quickly and that she was certain that he could produce a PowerPoint presentation on demand without any further support from her. I found this to be a very simple and elegant demonstration of complex overlapping zones of proximal development supported by a rich learning environment that included technology learning and art appreciation.

Diverse Age Grouping

Shelby decided to work with two preschool age children, her nephews, aged five and three years old. She decided to create a lesson for them on the computer related to healthy eating. As the two children interacted with her, discussing what they liked about certain foods and what foods were good and what foods would not be so good, the younger child made comments that the older child found informative. During her presentation she discussed how she realized that both children despite the age difference were performing "a head taller" than the other in different ways. The older child was able to absorb information and talk about it in a way that the younger child was able to creatively imitate. The younger child was able to ask interesting questions that provoked the older child in a similar direction. Shelby came away with the understanding that there were zones of proximal development and that the more diversity there was in the learning environment the richer the learning environment. She had not realized that a younger child had something to offer in this experience and came away with a significant development in her perspective.

Supporting Passion and Interest

Anna struggled with this assignment in terms of my direction to the class which was pursue your interests and your passions and bring them into an educational context. Anna had a hard time figuring out what her passions were, she could not recall anyone ever asking her the question. In light of her struggle I directed her to find some children and ask them what their passions were and see what the result was. When she returned to me she said she hadn't found much. I pressed her on what that meant and she started to describe her nephews aged 14 and 11. Both did well in school and both had interests outside of school. She learned that the 11 year old was interested in politics and was very engaged in political media. He used his parents as resources; he listened to their political conversations and asked them to take him to the library so that he could research his interests. She considered his passion for politics quite unusual. The older nephew had an interest in music but wasn't satisfied with the way he was learning music in his music class. He found what he was required to practice "babyish" and he had fears concerning taking on a different role in the classroom such as demonstrating how pieces should be played. Anna indicated that he seemed to have self-doubt and sensitivity to peer criticism. Anna's project became about whether or not these passions that her nephews had could be supported in school. It was no surprise to me when she reported back that neither of these children was being supported in a way that they could experience their passion in school. So my question to Anna became "What would you suggest be done for these students if you were devising an intervention with these teachers? What would you tell them to do with these kids?"

I suggested that she propose projects that were performatory and inclusive of others such as a news program that could be done during "current events." She developed her ideas and presented them to each of the children. Both children were enthusiastic about the ideas and both expressed hesitation around being singled out as the one who was doing something different or special. During her class presentation Anna raised these issues and her peers were very helpful in suggesting that the activities be organized as group activities that everybody was participating in as opposed to an activity where certain special members were being singled out. Being singled out exposed students to the pressure of having different interests from everyone else. Anna and the rest of us discovered that bringing passions and interests in to school is challenging because diverse interests can lead to feelings of isolation or exclusion if the group is not prepared to support it.

Adult Learning

Kate's project involved creating a workshop for two groups of adult students she had worked with over the past few months. Kate teaches adults basic computer skills and how to use the PowerPoint application. She invited students from her beginner level class and her intermediate level class to join her for a session where they worked together to complete a PowerPoint project. She indicated that what was interesting about the two different classes was that they were intentionally organized as "beginner" and "intermediate" because in adult education settings there is a lot of concern about making the students feel comfortable. Homogeneous grouping as determined by ability is a strategy for addressing issues related to anxiety. During her presentation Kate shared that in the readings assigned to the class she came to understand that a heterogeneous mixing of abilities in the classroom should create zones of proximal development where the more experienced students could support the less experienced students to perform "a head taller" than they would be able to without the assistance of more experienced others. A big concern of hers was creating an environment where everybody was comfortable and so to do that she played an improvisation game at the beginning of the workshop. She reported that the improvisation game was fun, people laughed, some people struggled trying to get the moves right. She reported that they were so committed to playing the game correctly that it was funny to watch and it created a shared experience where people came through their discomfort together. Kate's workshop went very well and she was very surprised at the level of collaboration that went on around her. She even stated that at one point she experienced being unnecessary to what was going on. She said that she felt that she had to insert herself into conversations and group work simply to have something to do. Kate reported that the game had had a significant impact on the mood in the classroom and it had created an environment where people felt comfortable. She was surprised at how the interactions between the beginners and the intermediate students became so productive and how the productivity of the students went beyond the paired groupings to the more general interactions between groups. She thought that the experience had implications for how she would run the training in the future. She mentioned introducing the possibility of playing the improvisation games to get the adults comfortable in class and perhaps doing more collaborative work in the adult training workshops.

Looking for Effects

Suzy decided that she wanted to see if there was an effect to playing improvisation games in the classroom that was readily observable. She organized an observation session where the cooperating teacher prepared by reading about improvisation games from the book *Unscripted Learning* and selected games from the book to play with her 3rd grade class as part of a math lesson. Suzy video recorded the performance and then edited the video and submitted it as evidence of her work. The video showed her talking to some kids before the lesson and getting the general feelings about their comfort level in the class and their feelings about math. The teacher that Suzy was working with was known to be a good teacher and that was evident in the video. The teacher carried out the games with the students and afterwards reported that the mood had changed but there was no evidence that this mood had an impact on learning.

During the discussion after Suzy's presentation she noted that it was very hard to tell what effect, if any, the game had on the overall activity of math learning in the classroom. We noted during the discussion that changing the mood in an environment is a significant effect and that we are quick dismiss being able to change the mood in the classroom as insignificant to learning. Suzy speculated that perhaps it would have been better to work with the teacher who wasn't so competent and that perhaps there would be a more pronounced effect in that situation. I reminded Suzy that I and many other teachers have used improvisation games in classrooms and that I could report to her that a less able teachers might struggle to pull off the game.

During our discussion I tried to contrast what Suzy had experienced as an observer in the classroom to what Kate had experienced as the teacher in her classroom. Suzy's cooperating teacher had no investment in improvisation or performance other than to try out a new method and even so the new method was successful in "changing the mood." Kate achieved what she perceived as "transformation." She had invested in creating an environment where the game had the effect of changing the emotional environment by creating a shared experience.

She experienced that transformation in part by realizing that she had re-created her role and that her job as she understood it had significantly changed. That Kate could report a significant effect from using the approaches that we had discussed was connected to the way she participated in the activity. Suzy's investment in the activity as an interested observer limited her experience. She could not report an effect because she had not participated in creating an effect to report on. Her work in this area provided a wonderful illustration on how to approach this work as an invested participant and creator, while highlighting the limitations of traditional approaches to research as they pertained to the performatory social therapeutic approaches being discussed in our course.

Facebook Recitals

Alan is a musician and an experienced music teacher. His project was partly inspired by the accounts in an earlier chapter on how Jessie used the Internet and YouTube videos to learn how to play the guitar. When he was formulating his project I suggested that he explore what he might do given that he was a music teacher and that students or people who are interested in playing the guitar were turning to the Internet for support. Alan conceived of a Facebook page that his students used to upload videos of performance pieces that he was teaching them during their private music lessons with him. The result was a series of videos from his students performing music ranging from classical to rock. Alan reported a high level of enthusiasm among his students for the project. Most interestingly he reported that the students seem to be listening to themselves on their videos more critically and "listening deeper." What he meant by that was that they were listening for their timing, they were realizing and commenting on how they were slowing down in the middle of certain pieces or going too fast or identifying very subtle aspects of their playing in a way that hadn't happened before. I consider this to be a significant finding. The technology integration was more than a process that might stand in for part of the practice-rehearsal-recital cycle; there was a qualitative improvement in that process. The students did something different and had a different experience, they became more than they could if left to their own practice of being musicians. Alan also had the unanticipated experience of getting support from some of his students who had a great deal of skill with video editing and producing and uploading the videos to the website.

Assessment

The projects and the learning presented here are as diverse as the students who produced them. I was thrilled with the results that my students produced. I think that our group had a transformational experience, we did things that we had not done before. I believe there is sufficient evidence in their reflections, in their project work and in their online interactions for me to conclude that they learned, developed new skills and that they developed socially and emotionally. They came to see things differently. Some of their long-held ideas about learning and teaching were at least called into question. Alan's final comment to me by way of taking his leave of the course was to state that he had learned some things that he had not expected to learn. I was deeply appreciative of his comment because I felt the same way. My students turned out to be a delightful group and I enjoyed working with them very much.

HIGHLIGHTS

- The experience of working with adults enrolled in a teacher certification program is presented.
- Student work is presented as a reflection on their experiences in working with the author on incorporating performatory approaches and technology integration into teaching practices.
- The student work provides evidence that working with technology and raising questions about pedagogical approaches brought about changes in their thinking about teaching and learning in classrooms.
- Students who performed for Facebook recitals demonstrated critical listening skills upon review of their video performances.
- Traditional research tools may be inappropriate for evaluating performatory learning environments.

QUESTIONS FOR DISCUSSION

1. What are some ideas that you have for designing a learning experience?
2. How do you see creating a learning experience in the context of creating a learning environment?
3. How do you approach students who struggle with an assignment?
4. How do you evaluate diverse student responses when they "reflect" on what they have learned?
5. What are your thoughts on passions and interests in school-based learning?

TEACHER – RESEARCHER

The research that I do is inseparable from my teaching practice. My teaching practice includes my training in performance and social therapy and my experience as a corporate technology professional. It's all inseparable and part of my history. My wife once asked, "how does it all go together?" It was a good question. It stumped me for 5 seconds and then I said, "it's what I do, and that's how it goes together. "

A researcher who was discussing my work with me asked how the approach I was advocating addressed learning school subjects like math. I explained that I believed that school subjects were separated from the lived experiences of school children. My observation is that they didn't understand why they were asked to learn certain things and how those things were connected to their lives. Through performances, such as project work, model building, programming and play, just to name a few, what is learned is happening in the context of the activity students are engaged in. In some traditional approaches to learning students are required to know a subject in the absence of experiences. When we create a school subject like math, we separate it from doing math as an activity in life. This separation or alienation of the subject from relevant lived experiences makes the subject into an abstraction. Performance re-establishes the dialectical unity of activity and the things that can be learned (Holzman, 2009).

My ongoing investigations are no more and no less than trying to *create learning environments where there is meaningful activity and opportunities to learn.* My interventions are attempts at engaging groups of learners in a process that may result in many different kinds of learning. Seeing ourselves as performers develops our capacity to respond to change and learn new things. If we can change "I can't do math!" to "I can perform doing math!" at some point, within a group context, we will actually learn to do math. Performance helps to transform "I can't."

A key focus of many school reform efforts is improving the quality of teaching by improving the teachers. There are two tools for doing this. The first is the school of education and teacher certification programs that produces the teachers. The second tool is known as professional development for teachers who are already in schools. Let's take a look at the attitudes that some teachers may hold regarding professional development, I must admit that earlier in my career my attitude was not much different from those expressed by my fictional peers.

Setting: A school cafeteria in the South Bronx, during a professional development half-day. Two teachers are sitting at the lunch table talking during a peer-sharing moment in the training. A university research group is leading the PD.

Ms. Jones:	*Really, how do they expect me to stop what I am doing to implement their proven methods?*
Mr. Franklin:	*Tell me about it, they don't come in and teach these kids in a real teaching environment, they have 5 adults standing around watching them do their method with a kid or a small group of kids. How realistic is that?*
Ms. Jones:	*They don't deal with the other 35 students and all the interruptions and all the other stuff. I don't know how their results are proven.*
Mr. Franklin:	*All I know is that they never tried their methods with these kids in a real schooling situation like this.*
Ms. Jones:	*I did one of these grant projects before. With all the extra resources you start to make a dent and then their grant finishes. They go away to write a paper. There you are maybe a little smarter but right back where you started with no resources and no support.*

There is a great deal of good research being done by researchers in classrooms. However, the basic critique rings true, the researchers will leave when the grant money ends and the support that they provided will leave with them. The sustainability of the new practices they introduced within the classroom becomes highly dependent on individuals and not the institution.

Research activity requires time to read, reflect and dialogue with peers and mentors. The typical teacher has no time to do any of these activities during the normal school day and very little time during the week. Most teachers I know spend a significant portion of their personal time checking student work, planning the next lesson and responding to administrative demands. Add in time for family and friends and other personal responsibilities and there simply isn't time to be a reflective teacher-researcher. Something has to give. My time in grad school was stressful and I made sacrifices gave up, income, entertainment, weekends, time with family, socializing and sleep. I with a lot of support I became a much better teacher.

I think that every teacher should be a researcher. I don't think that every teacher needs to have a doctorate. Educational institutions must support teachers to be more sophisticated in their approaches as a basic requirement for 21st century teaching and learning. My feeling is that a redesigned school day and school year is necessary to support teachers to research and develop their teaching practices.

The Development Gap

What I find most outrageous about the current state of affairs in schooling is that doing better is expressed as reforms that emphasize increasing efficiency and gathering more data through the use of technology. Efforts toward creating learning environments that are humane, equitable, relevant and developmental don't seen to get much press. In their white paper All Stars Project co-founder Lenora Fulani and president Gabrielle Kurlander refer to this as the development gap (Fulani & Kurlander, 2009) that policy makers and administrators have been unable to close with their focus on the achievement gap.

My initial interest in schooling and subsequent immersion in schools as a teacher was with the intent of understanding how the system worked so that I could have a hand in fixing it. As I began to understand the workings of public education I abandoned the idea of fixing it. We need to build something new.

While I believe that the education system needs to be replaced, I also recognize that it is what we have for the foreseeable future. The business leaders and politicians who have a stake in education and have been engineering education policy for the purpose of national economic development and national security (Spring, 2006) have failed at achieving an educational system where the needs of all students are met and the goals that we set are reached. Their question is, "How do we increase student achievement for the purpose of reaching the goals that we set?" That question assumes that a deficit must be addressed.

In a radio interview (Wertheimer, 2010) during the spring of 2010, Margaret Spellings, the Secretary of Education during the Bush Administration and one of the designers of the No Child Left Behind Act (NCLB), said that America needed to educate people to higher levels in order to lead the world in innovation. She indicated that this priority was in the interest of national security, economic security and being competitive in a global knowledge economy. When asked early in the interview about "teaching to the test" she indicated that as long as the test could measure the knowledge we required students to have, she saw no flaw in the pedagogical approach. The context for the interview was to solicit her thoughts on the Obama administration's plan to change NCLB. One of the key proposals of the plan was to dismiss the teachers at chronically under-performing schools (as an approach to creating change), or what was described as the bottom 10 percent of schools. With their deficit perspectives intact (we'll fix it by getting rid of low performers), educational change leaders will continue to present incremental reforms as their approach to improving education, this is an example the development gap that Fulani and Kurlander are pointing to.

A Good Profession

Some of my students have been justifiably concerned about the profession that they were preparing for. Given the current state of affairs, it would be reasonable to become discouraged. In fact, I sometimes wondered what I was preparing teacher candidates for. In spite of my dislike and criticism of the education system, I'm hopeful. I believe that my job is to provide others with tools that they can be creative with. I also hope to influence teachers that I work with to be critical of what they are presented with and open to new ideas. I believe being both open and critical is part of being innovative and creative in any attempt to create or respond to change. My students have demanded that I be more explicit by what I mean and so what follows is my attempt to be more explicit.

Creating Passions and Interests

My interest in education, as I have described in these pages, was created. I didn't have an interest or passion in education for most of my life. My activity in different communities created my desire to invest in my own learning. I participated in formal (graduate school and training programs) and informal (volunteering at non-profits) learning environments. It has been very significant to me that my informal learning experiences were of equal and sometimes superior quality to the formal learning experiences. That was possible because I surrounded myself with educators who also happened to be very diverse and had expertise across many disciplines. I have been, and continue to be, immersed in communities of practice such as those found at the East Side Institute, the All Stars Project, and the CUNY Graduate Center that are committed to creating developmental learning environments. My membership in different communities provides me with colleagues that support my interests and provides the opportunity to learn about and support the interests of others.

The Activity: Create the Environment

In order to do something new you have to go out of your way to create environment where something new is possible. I've spent the last 15 years of my life trying to understand why it's that simple to articulate and so difficult to accomplish. You have to take responsibility for the fact that in well-established environments people are going to resist change and they will resist individuals and groups who champion change.

In the area of getting teachers to use technology, I do not target teachers who don't use technology. I find teachers who are interested in technology and eliminate the barriers (no equipment, broken equipment, lack of access, fear) to using the technology. This group is not resistant they will welcome help, ideas, encouragement and resources. The goal, over time, is to create an environment where everyone has an expectation that technology integration is something that is done in school. It's easier said than done, but possible nonetheless. The process of creating the environment creates more development, more creativity, and more possibilities. Will the people who resisted technology change their minds? Maybe. It depends on a lot factors, one of them being an interest in participating in what everyone else is doing. If you get a significant number of teachers, students and parents invested in using technology and support them to do so the fact of a few holdouts ceases to be a barrier in efforts to move forward.

Relationships: Relate to Groups

Our current model of education is based on relating to individuals and yet those individuals find themselves in groups and quite often are not prepared to be able to relate to groups or other members of the group. If you've come this far you've already committed to beginning the additional work and study on how to relate to groups This will require more than reading up on cooperative and collaborative learning. The critical element is finding a group to be part of that is committed to becoming a better group, a developing group (Holzman and Mendez, 2003). That group may be your grade team, or a professional organization outside of school. It doesn't matter what the goal of the group is, what matters is that you're having the experience of being part of a group that is looking for ways to improve itself. It's actually hard to find groups with this orientation, most groups that I've been a part of exist to achieve goals in the short term and development of the group is secondary if it is acknowledged at all.

The most helpful book that I found in the area of creating and developing groups is *Psychological Investigations* edited by Holzman and Mendez. They present many of the dialogues between Fred Newman and the therapists he trained. Those dialogues are relevant and salient to the approach to pedagogy discussed in this book. Many of the pedagogical issues that are raised for leaders (therapists, teachers, performers, trainers) who are working to support groups are discussed in depth.

Design Learning Experiences

Most lesson plans and unit plans are designed to produce uniform outcomes for students. In other words, all the students are supposed to acquire at least the minimum knowledge of content during the course of a lesson or unit plan and then produce evidence of their knowledge. A standardized measure is used to determine whether they have achieved a satisfactory level of mastery but it will not indicate whether they mastered more than was required. At best this type of measure will identify those who did and did not master what was required.

I think we can do a little better if we design learning experiences for groups and provide them with open-ended slightly ambiguous assignments. Project-based learning is a good enough area to start. Project-based learning defines a project for students to work towards accomplishing as a group. There is a significant body of literature on project-based learning, and there are specific requirements for doing it "correctly" with an interest in knowledge acquisition as a final outcome. I believe there is an opportunity here to use technology to facilitate open-ended inquiry and creativity even within the formal structures of project-based learning. What I have done in my classes is attempt to design learning experiences that are not merely about what knowledge students must acquire but also to a create forums (electronic or in person) to share what the experience was like and support dialogues about the social and emotional and cultural aspects of group learning environments. The dialogues have helped me more closely align what was being taught with students' life experiences and interests, I believe this has led to richer the experiences for all of us.

When I've introduced choices and broadened how we related to content and the process of creating projects I've found that I could be more demanding and more sensitive to student concerns. What has been effective for me is instituting a project proposal process where students can have an ongoing interaction with me about their ideas and we work together towards the goal of persuading me to approve the project. Another obstacle is that some students find the prospect of identifying their own project overwhelming and are unable to generate ideas. To address this I usually provide a list of project ideas and I encourage students to become part of a group that is doing something they have an interest in.

Create A New Teacher Performance

Most teachers come to know that one of the first things they need to do with their students is to form positive relationships. Every one of us has to make decisions about what the nature of those relationships will be. Those relationships all happen within the context of the school that we are working in. The teaching practices of those around us influence us. Our students and their parents also influence us. In a school where there are many problematic teaching practices new teachers unavoidably acquire some of the bad practices. These are the things that make up a teacher performance. This is why I advocate for forming relationships outside of the school. Teachers need more and varied input to the process of creating their new teacher performances.

Focusing on doing new things in a school, like technology, creates opportunities for professional development outside of the school or will bring experienced educators into the school. A common component of professional development around technology is to make best practices available. I don't believe that a "best practice" should be a goal. I see best practices as a step in the direction of mastery and becoming an innovative practitioner. Standard best practices are important but there is nothing that is innovative or creative about them. I believe that we should be creating a community of learners who believe that they can learn and create (innovate) what they need. A dynamic balance between standardization and innovation needs to be maintained.

I have discovered the value of creating environments where individuals in groups are constantly given opportunities to create new relationships and develop those relationships in positive ways. This means focusing on the group, creating more opportunities to collaborate, and creating new expectations. For example, you can't have collaborative project-based environments if students are expected to be quiet and remain in their seats all day long. You cannot expect people to collaborate and not argue about something. You have to invest yourself in learning how to support people to disagree in a principled ways. This is true whether or not the relationship is between you and your students or you and your administration. You have to find ways to disagree in a principled way without making the issue personal, even if you feel that "they are making it personal." This is one of the most challenging proposals in this book, learning the "yes, and" of improvisation and performance training is critical to being able to move forward in building a new teacher performance.

Assessing Development

What I care about, when I am working to create the learning environment is creating opportunities for people to try new things. Students who take up an offer to try something new are taking a step in their development. When students start to create their own opportunities to try new things are making an even bigger leap in development. Those who engage others in their development are developing themselves and the communities that they live in. This is what happens in the youth development programs of the All Stars Project and it is the kind of learning environment that might be assessed using non-traditional tools (Gordon, Bowman, & Mejia, 2003).

I have found that development in the short term is easier to see in a group. On the first day of school not many kids are talking, by the end of the day they are all chatting with each other as if they had been friends forever. That is, if you've given them a chance to talk at all! The formation of new relationships is a sign of development. Engagement in new activities is another. Imagine that the students are playing in small groups in the play yard and you suggest a large group game of freeze tag. The game goes well and the next time you observe that the children organize their own game of freeze tag. The group is demonstrating the ability to organize its own activity this is another sign of development.

A group that works together well as a group is qualitatively different than the group of children who cannot work as a group. There are clear signs of social and emotional development in the group of children who can cooperate and collaborate that are desirable. The challenge is in responding to the question: How do we create and sustain the group? I've discovered that technology is helpful in creating more possibilities for new kinds of interactions in and out of the classroom and interactions are necessary for creating and supporting groups of learners.

Philosophizing

Take ordinary everyday occurrences and ask big questions about the little things. Do you understand that yelling at Johnny to sit down is more about how you are feeling than about Johnny breaking the rules? Is Freddy's calling out and disrupting in the back of the room simply an example of him being a behavior problem or is it a critique of the teaching that is going on? Does closing your door and "doing what you need to do" improve your teaching? These are some questions that you might pose if you are seriously considering trying to change the repetitive scripts that play out in schools everyday. I have found that philosophizing, having a dialogue, about how we use language and how we participate in activities and relationships helps in bringing about the possibility of change. When we philosophize we allow ourselves to question the meanings of the words that we use and the assumptions that go along with them. The practice of social therapy features the philosophizing activity and has been proven to be helpful to groups of people who are stuck in the confusion that may be brought about in the everyday, taken for granted, use of language (Newman & Holzman, 1997). We don't need to become therapists or be in therapy to philosophize, but we do need to take responsibility for our interactions with others and I have discovered that making change, trying to improve what goes on in schools, means challenging strongly held, taken for granted assumptions about the way things are.

Bringing Change

I've discovered that in order to bring change to an environment you have to be willing to change. You have to be willing to change *your understanding* of how rules, constraints, resources and perceptions impact you and how they impose on your relationships with your students. When you act on making a change you are venturing into the unknown.

Play can be used to create an environment where everyone is participating in taking on the unknown, where it's possible to have a good time and where people are learning how to work in a group. Creative and imaginative play is available for younger students in schools and is harder to schedule with older students, but not impossible. Introducing play activities into a literacy block for older students can be awkward and uncomfortable for everyone.

A significant and unexpected learning experience for me was that I became vulnerable to my students and peers as I introduced performance and play into my teaching. I saw that their performances (responses to what I did) had an impact on my performances and emotions and I saw that I needed to make choices about what I valued. The underdeveloped (negative and blaming) teaching performances around us can create unpleasant, if not destructive situations. A typical response, in my experience, of teachers who disagree what is going on around them is to close the classroom door. The most development in my teaching occurred when play, performance and open-ended project work took place in front of the broadest audience (Parents, students, teachers and administrators). When I finally "opened my classroom door" and let everyone in I achieved transparency in my teaching practice and by doing so I was able to have a greater impact on the learning community I was part of. By the time I made that move I had done the work that was necessary to address critiques and challenges to what I was doing.

Advocating for a new methodological approach to teaching and learning or taking a chance on integrating new technology in a classroom places new kinds of demands on the teacher. Actively organizing within your peer group or learning community and creating support for your organizing activities is necessary to maintain your credibility and standing. I decided to get a Ph.D. and volunteer extensively with organizations that used the approach that I was interested in, this was how I approached my development in the interest of creating change. How you approach yours will be different. What I have put forth here are the concrete things that I have done. What follows is brief collection of dialogues and comments that I have heard from teachers while talking about using technology in the classroom.

TALKING ABOUT TECHNOLOGY IN SCHOOLS

Various educators have made the following comments or raised following questions in conversations that I participated in.

"...it's [technology] an extension of the classroom."

It is an oversimplification to simply claim that online environments can extend the classroom. Online environments can provide opportunities to interact and access resources that would not otherwise be possible in a "classroom." The "classroom" ceases to be a well-defined place where students show up to learn, it becomes a place with blurry boundaries where students work in groups and participate in complex social interactions that would not be possible without technology. Online environments, used imaginatively, can transform what is possible for teachers and students.

"How do I get what I want?" (In the case students learning curriculum)

It is reasonable to use technology in a way that will result in predetermined outcomes but this alone does not lead to transformation, it's automation of learning tasks. Designing learning tasks in open-ended ways for groups helps to counterbalance the tendency to automate.

"It just won't fit in to my schedule"

This is a very typical response to many professional development initiatives that require teachers to add to what they already do in the classroom. Whether the "it" is a performance game or a new technology the initial reaction seems to be related to a teacher having to do more work within a fixed time frame. The notion of a learning environment, as I have developed it, is not limited to the physical space provided by a classroom or the resources in it, nor does it need to limit responsibility for what goes on to a single teacher. Creating an environment where there is distributed leadership and responsibility is the key to making "it fit." I would also suggest, examining existing practices and checking to see if they are not outdated or obsolete, discontinuing those practices may also create space to make innovation "fit."

"I'm just walking around and monitoring"

In a learning environment that has online content and regular access to wireless laptops in which the students are engaged in collaborative learning what is the role of the teacher? It is easy to fall into the mode of walking around, monitoring for "on task" behavior and answering questions as the expert. Multimedia Internet technologies can accommodate the needs of diverse learners. A dynamic learning environment where interactions include more than simple questions and answers is possible if the teacher is no longer merely a monitor of behavior or a transmitter of information. The "expertise" of the teacher can be provided in the context of a providing direction to the group as it engages in learning activities. The teacher becomes a director, coach, manager or producer as he or she walks around and attempts to engage students in conversations about their work, passions, interests and progress with the task at hand.

"I need to know how before I do this with a kid."

Human beings regularly demonstrate that they have the capacity to relate to each other without always having the benefit of "knowing how" prior to doing something. For example, babies don't know anything prior to becoming speakers of a language. The practical challenge for implementing new methodologies and technologies in the classroom is in re-initiating development in teachers so that they can work in collaboration with students who "already know" about technology.

"Books and literacy are still important."

Books and literacy are important and Internet discussion forums that permit users to provide their own content for public display and interaction can produce texts that contain many simultaneous voices (polyphonic) (Bakhtin, 1981). The use of discussion forums in learning environments creates new opportunities for literacy, interaction with content, reflection and change in the classroom. New concepts in student literacy are possible as image, threaded discussion, hyperlinked text, digital video, digital audio and messaging systems become tools in the production of content and interactions with others.

"I still think it's about the parents."

We can certainly use technology to reach out to parents in new ways and provide them with more access to what goes on in school. We can use the idea of building groups to create a more inclusive dialogue with parents about the education of their children. The pervasive sentiment that public education fails or succeeds in its task because of parent involvement is beyond our scope. In my view, the task for the teacher is to work with what is available and to bring as much transparency and critical thought to his or her practices as possible.

"This is all well and good, but I am preparing kids for the real world."

My central claim is this: In using technology and a performatory social therapeutic approach as tools in the creation of learning environments in school I became a better teacher. The narratives and vignettes are as much about the changes in my practices as they are about the changes in students that I interacted with. I base my practices on theoretical frameworks that were developed over the course of 30 years in partnership with young people who were growing up in the boroughs of New York City. The All Stars Project and the East Side Institute are non-profits that have survived every economic downturn of the last 30 years and currently have affiliates that can be found in other cities and have strong ties to educators and therapists in other countries. All of this was accomplished independently of government funding. Ordinary people have made these programs possible and have funded and supported these projects with volunteer efforts. The programs that the All Stars Project provides to young people free of charge help them to learn developmentally "in the real world." They are not different kids from the ones in the inner city public schools, they are the very same students who have experienced failure and frustration in public schools for all the reasons, poverty, gang violence, poor parenting, poor teachers, etc. that you care to name. Performatory approaches to human learning and development are producing positive results for people all over the world. The Internet and multimedia technologies allow us to form and sustain new relationships and to hear, see and create new activities as we engage others. I've developed, I've presented my evidence, and it is my hope that you recognize that supporting the development of others is developmental and helps us to create the "real world."

IMPLICATIONS

My teaching practices developed using a performatory social therapeutic approach and I have created and supported a complex cultural environment in technology rich classrooms. My willingness to "accept offers" and see students as performers rather than people with fixed identities, behaviors and/or disabilities, opened up creative possibilities for further engagement. The highly scripted interactions that ended in negative feelings and lost opportunities to build learning environments were disrupted by improvisation, technology and a commitment to a way of being in a group that valued inclusiveness, diversity, democracy and fairness. The bureaucratized discourse of schools was disrupted when "teaching to" students was re-framed as "performing with." Power, leadership and authority became distributed. The groups I worked with developed the capacity to create and take responsibility for thier own learning. The contradictions that were glossed over in the daily routine of schooling became much harder to ignore when student performances and commitments to building community were experienced by me as collaborative activity.

I believe that the totality of learning environments can be transformed when students and teachers have new technologies to interact with and the flexibility to create new collaborative learning activities. Increased opportunities to communicate and interact introduced higher demands in navigating the many-to-many relationships that were possible when hundreds of students started using discussion forums for their own purposes. Satisfaction and frustration were produced for all of us when we used technology in the classroom. Sometimes we experienced both of those strong emotions within the same minute. I was surprised to experience a wide range of emotional responses to how technologies are used to restrict or manage activity, and what the technology could do to further our public and private agendas. Issues such as online bullying became more apparent but equally visible were the kindness, generosity and playfulness that were also happening online when open ended public discussion forums and Internet technologies were made available in conjunction with commitments to providing leadership to developmental learning environments.

SOME DEVELOPING IDEAS

As we close in on the last few pages of this book I would like to leave you with some ideas that I am interested in pursuing and some closing thoughts. I don't want to leave you with the impression that anything has ended or that we have come to some sort of conclusion. Creating learning environments using technology and a performatory social therapeutic approach to teaching and learning is the open-ended project that I have given myself and the way I see it, there is much more to do. In this book I have presented my methodology, rationale, and my experience. As the curtain drops, here are some ideas. Make them your own, join me in pursuing them, or create your own. We have the tools to create new kinds of learning environments for our students and I hope that this book will help you to do so.

Student Production of Educational Content

Communities of scholars use publications and digital artifacts to share information and build the practices of the community. Increasingly inexpensive technologies such as digital video cameras, and open source software make it possible to support students to publish and distribute multimedia documents, audio streams and video. Using performatory approaches to the process of production in math, science and literacy classrooms may provide a relevant content archive for an online learning community.

Interventions in mathematics or science classrooms would require outside facilitators who would work with students to develop social and emotional dimensions of content learning. Outside volunteers or college interns could be used to facilitate the production of videos. Materials and "how to" instructional videos might be made available through an online course component. Teachers and students could then be supported to reflect on the contents of the videos and work toward the development of content that is meaningful and supportive of learning in the school community. Achieving a higher level of student engagement is the starting point of a process that requires students to have greater input into the selection of technology dependent projects. The process would include more extensive peer review and accountability to the learning community.

Online Collaboration for Learning Communities

For the foreseeable future the school day will continue to be organized around set curricula, testing regimes and data driven instruction. Social Networking and online discussion forums that are driven by student interests may provide a means for positive interactions that can disrupt "question and answer routines" of the classroom without taking up "class time." These environments can also provide new avenues for disrupting other intractable learning problems by providing the means for students to have contact with outside educators who are removed from the day-to-day in-school issues that can impede learning. Online teachers could provide a different perspective on students to the in-school faculty. A key feature of producing this environment is providing students with the means to determine the direction of the online discussions and training teachers to participate in expanding and directing those discussions. This type of environment would serve to ignite student interests and passions, which could then be supported.

School-based Social Networking and Social Media

Technology is increasing the number of interactions that students and teachers have as they come into contact with each other and the communities in which they are situated. From my own experience I have witnessed how school administrators struggle to address the issues that arise from online interactions. School policies currently favor lockdown scenarios (no social networks) and appropriate use policies as a response to the transparency and porosity that the Internet creates at school. I would argue that a new paradigm for training in the area of emotional, social and community development is necessary to support school communities that are struggling to control online student interactions and parent-teacher-administrator interactions. Teachers are ill-served when they are positioned as the gatekeepers of Internet activity. Instead of banning social networking and social media, schools need to make use of these technologies for engaging all stakeholders in dialogues about their interests in the community. Increased interaction with the broader community would be a first step toward greater transparency in school level and district level decision making. A key to supporting creative dialogue among a broad audience of stakeholders would be to identify and train community facilitators or leaders to engage issues as they come up without playing "the blame game." Students and teachers would benefit from participating in a public space where learning how to "social network" responsibly was a basic requirement for participating in a 21st century learning community.

A Curriculum for Creating and Designing

I've observed that young people are highly competent users of technology that is designed to be easy to use but many have no idea as to how any of it works. The time might be right for introducing basic computer programming as part of the elementary and secondary school curriculum. Computer programming courses contain aspects of science, mathematics, literacy, and the basic concepts that are necessary for understanding how a broad range of technologies work. Programming environments for children have become easier to use and have been enabled with engaging multimedia elements. Programming is also a creative activity that is ultimately done in groups as the programming challenges become more complex. I think many young people who struggle with traditional approaches to learning may benefit from engaging in programming and design activities. The fields of computational thinking, robotics and game design seem to be making progress in this area and are sources of rich content and educational tools.

Performatory Social Therapeutic Approaches to Support Development In Communities

For the last 30 years the All Star Project has been successful in re-initiating the development of tens of thousands of young people and adults in New York City. In the last 15 years the All Stars Project has expanded to New Jersey, Boston, Chicago, San Francisco, Atlanta, and internationally in the Netherlands and Uganda. The All Stars Project and the East Side Institute served as my stages for development and those organizations exist to provide stages for young and not so young people to reinitiate development and build community. These are ongoing projects that sustain themselves financially without dependence on government funding. Their success is attributable to thousands of individuals who provide financial support for their youth development and education programs.

VALUES AND ETHICS

I believe that we have an obligation to try to create the best learning environments that we can, all of the time, for everyone. Aligning my teaching activities with my own interests and enthusiasm and committing to being an active member of different communities has contributed greatly to my development as a teacher and a human being.

I respectfully question what is commonly accepted as standard teaching practices within public schools. I disagree with much of what happens in education policy decision-making. That being stated, *creating agreements* among people who disagree on what constitutes the best learning environment possible seems to me to be the best route forward.

I have provided an account of planned and improvised approaches to creating learning environments that were consciously organized in ways that engaged students in taking risks, being reflective, pursing interests, assuming responsibilities and valuing participation with others. This was attempted as a way of creating a new classroom culture and making development possible. This resulted in teaching and learning practices were dynamic, accountable, responsive and relevant to the community.

Taking responsibility for the creation of new culture means also being mindful of the culture that is being produced and considering the audience (the community) and the impact of what is being produced (digital artifacts, new practices, new expectations). I have found that parents are both enthusiastic supporters of their children having broad experience with technology as a part of their schooling. They are also very concerned about the exposure of children to cyber bullying and the adult themes that the Internet and mass media afford. I believe that active support of the online and in-person technology-based activities of children is a necessary area of development for educators and parents.

The outside-of-school educators that had an impact on my life had autonomy and responsibility for organizing sustainable learning environments. Institutional support from outside of the school has been a key to my own development as a student and for my development as a teacher. I believe that providing teachers with institutional resources that are responsive to their interests and developmental needs can provide a route to change in the classroom. I also think that providing communities with new ways to relate to their schools via technology resources and a performatory approach to building communities might provide the incentives for change at the policy level that can support changes at the classroom level.

Technology is my vehicle for introducing a different approach to pedagogy into schools. As schools adopt technology we have an opportunity to introduce a new pedagogy based on proven collaborative approaches to human development and learning. Here's what I've learned: teaching is an intensely personal commitment to the well-being of others. That commitment is enacted in relationships that can give rise to learning environments that support the development of the learning community and are developed in the context of a learning community. What I have shared in this book is my approach to becoming a better teacher, improving education and changing the world.

HIGHLIGHTS

- The author summarizes his views and his values.
- Ideas or suggestions for future or ongoing projects are presented.
- The implications of a performatory social therapeutic approach in the classroom are discussed.
- The author responds to common questions or issues in implementing technology in the classroom.
- The author discusses the development gap in the context of creating a new dialogue about education.
- The author presents his stance on his performance of a teacher-researcher.

QUESTIONS FOR DISCUSSION

1. What are your views and values?
2. What do you see as the barriers to creating developmental learning environments?
3. What is your approach to pedagogy?
4. Who supports your efforts in the classroom?
5. How are you going to become a better teacher?
6. What tools will you need to create to support your own development?

GLOSSARY

This brief glossary is provided to clarify meanings of certain words or phrases that may be unfamiliar or used in unfamiliar ways in this book.

Alienation – From a Marxist standpoint, it's the separation or isolation of a person from others or the things that people create or produce.

Creative imitation – A type of performance where the learner is performing a role that she or he is not yet qualified to do. An example would be young children pretending to be the parent or the teacher during imaginative play. This type of performance is also important in language development, babies perform as speakers before they learn to speak.

Deconstruct – A form of analysis that attempts to find hidden contradictions or assumptions.

Development – A process that features growth or the ability to do something that was previously beyond ability.

Developmental learning – An approach to learning where performed activity and play are featured as critical to social, emotional and cognitive development.

Dialectics – An approach to reasoning that starts with a contradiction and is considered a source of development from a Marxist standpoint. This method supports seeing things that are typically considered as separate or opposite as unities.

Dualism – An approach to reasoning that identifies things as separate or in contrast such as mind and body or teaching and learning.

Ethnography – Descriptions of the lives and customs of people that are being observed and interacted with from an observer's point of view. Auto-ethnography describes aspects of your own life from within the social context that is of interest. The methods of ethnography include storytelling via vignettes, narratives, anecdotes, critical reflections, and analysis from a theoretical perspective. Ethnography has become a qualitative tool in education research and the social sciences.

Historical context – Refers to the social cultural setting of a particular event.

Knowledge acquisition learning – Learning for the purpose of demonstrating mastery of facts without direct experience of those facts. This type of learning depends on the ability of the learner to remember facts and information and communicate about facts and information appropriately.

Learning environment – An environment that is created for the purpose of supporting learners to engage in activities that result in learning.

Performance – A task or activity that is engaged in by performer. There is typically an audience or the idea of an audience that the performance is for. A greeting, standing in line for a cup of coffee and singing in a talent show are all examples of a performance.

Improvisation – An unscripted performance that requires creative collaboration or innovation on the part of the performer(s).

Qualitative Inquiry – A concern with the methodological approach to qualitative research.

Qualitative Research – An approach to inquiry that is concerned with particular cases that are being studied. The data of qualitative research is found in the narratives, vignettes and stories of people and events. Video recordings and other types of artifacts are also used in qualitative research. Social science researchers typically use interdisciplinary approaches in this type of research.

Social therapy – A form of group therapy pioneered by Fred Newman and developed in collaboration with Lois Holzman and others. The social therapeutic framework is based on Newman and Holzman's practices and synthesis of the methodological approaches of Karl Marx, Lev Vygotsky's contributions in the field of psychology and Ludwig Wittgenstein's contributions in philosophy.

Tool and result – The simultaneous creation of a tool and a result. Most tools are created to produce a particular result, tools for results, and may be reused appropriately to produce identical results. Tool and result types of tools are custom made for a particular circumstance. A hammer is a tool for result tool. An improvisational performance is a tool and result type of tool.

Underdeveloped – In this context underdeveloped describes an ability or social situation that has not benefited from circumstances that would promote growth.

Way of being – Ontology or how we are in the world.

REFERENCES

Bakhtin, M. M. (1981). *The dialogic imagination: Four essays by M. M. Bakhtin* (C. Emerson & M. Holquist, Trans.). Austin, TX: University of Texas Press.

Csikszentmihalyi, M. (1990). *Flow: The psychology of optimal experience.* New York: Harper Perennial.

Freire, P. (2003). *Pedagogy of the oppressed.* New York: Continuum International Publishing Co.

Fulani, L. B., & Kurlander, G. L. (2009). *Achievement gap or development gap?, "Outliers" and outsiders reconsider and old problem.* New York City: All Stars Project, Inc.

Gee, J. P. (2003). *What video games have to teach us about learning and literacy.* New York: Palgrave Macmillan.

Gonzales, J. (2000). *Harvest of empire: A history of Latinos in America.* Harmondsworth, Middlesex, England: Viking.

Gordon, E. W., Bowman, C. B., & Mejia, B. X. (2003). *Changing the script for youth development: An evaluation of the All Stars Talent Show Network and the Joseph A. Forgione Development School for Youth.* New York: Teachers College, Columbia University.

Holzman, L. (2006). What kind of theory is activity theory? Introduction. *Theory & Psychology, 16*(1), 5–11.

Holzman, L. (2009). *Vygotsky at work and play.* London: Routledge.

Holzman, L. (2011). How is pretending Vygotskian? Personal communication, Faculty at the East Side Institute, New York.

Holzman, L., & Mendez, R. (Eds.). (2003). *Psychological investigations: A clinician's guide to social therapy.* New York: Brunner-Routledge.

Lave, J., & Wenger, E. (1991). *Situated learning: Legitimate peripheral participation.* New York: Cambridge University Press.

Lobman, C., & Lundquist, M. (2007). *Unscripted learning: Using improv activities across the K-8 curriculum.* New York: Teachers College Press.

Mehan, H. (1988). Educational handicaps as a cultural meaning system. *Ethos, 16*(1), 73–91.

Mehan, H. (1993). Beneath the skin and between the ears: A case study in the politics of representation. In S. Chakilin & J. Lave (Eds.), *Understanding practice: Perspectives on activity and context* (pp. 241–268). Cambridge: Cambridge University Press.

Newman, F., & Holzman, L. (1993). *Lev Vygotsky: revolutionary scientist.* New York: Routledge.

Newman, F., & Holzman, L. (1997). *The end of knowing: A new developmental way of learning.* New York, NY: Routledge.

Spring, J. (2006). *Pedagogies of globalization: The rise of the educational security state.* Mahwah, NJ: Lawrence Erlbaum Associates.

Wertheimer, L. (2010). *Spellings: 'No Child Left Behind' is a 'Toxic Brand'.* Retrieved October 25, 2010, from http://www.npr.org/templates/story/story.php?storyId=124758597

Winsler, A., Abar, B., Feder, M. A., Schunn, C. D., & Rubio, D. A. (2007). Private speech and executive functioning among high-functioning children with autistic spectrum disorders. *Journal of Autism and Developmental Disorders, 37*(9), 1617–1635.

INDEX

Printed in the United States
By Bookmasters